Ask Marilyn

Bible Answers to Questions About Real Life

by Marilyn Hickey

P.O. Box 17340 • Denver, Colorado 80217

ASK MARILYN
Bible Answers to Questions About Real Life

P.O. Box 17340
Denver, Colorado 80217

ISBN 1-56441-022-6

All scriptures are quoted from the *King James Version* of the Bible unless otherwise indicated.

CONTENTS

Chapter One

GOD AND THE BIBLE

Q. Why should I read the whole Bible?

A. The Bible is God's primary method of communicating with His creation, mankind. It is His revealed Word and will to man. Through reading and studying the Bible, you can meet, get to know, and establish a one-on-one relationship with the one true God, your Creator. As such, the Bible can be your best friend.

Its two major divisions, the Old Testament and the New Testament, both point to Jesus as the Redeemer of the human race. The Old Testament prepared the way for Jesus, and the New Testament prepares a people to receive Him.

That's why it's so important for you to read *every* book in the Bible—you can behold Jesus in every book of the Bible! Each book reveals to you Jesus and His love for you. When you read the whole Bible, you will recognize the unity of the Bible, and can apply its truths to every area of your life.

Q. How do you know God wrote the Bible?

A. The Bible claims God as its author, and a knowledge of the Word makes this apparent. There are 66 books in the Bible—written by more than 30 different persons over a period of thousands of years, and yet there is a consistent theme running from Genesis to Revelation. The Bible describes the fall of man, his utter sinfulness, and God's redemptive plan through the blood sacrifice of His Son. If the scriptures were not written by inspiration of the Holy Spirit, the mortal men who penned them surely would not present man as *totally* depraved and in need of salvation.

Man's "religion" always teaches access to God through human effort, but the Bible clearly states that mankind is dead in trespasses and sin. Dead men can't work their way to God; they can only accept God's provision of a new life in Christ Jesus.

Each of the prophets declared that it was the Word of the Lord that came to them; and with the exception of end-time prophecy, all prophecy has been fulfilled to the letter—even as God said it would be (II Timothy 3:15-17; II Peter 1:20,21).

Q. Is the Bible *really* God's infallible Word?

A. Yes, the Bible is God's infallible Word. Even though there are scriptures which, when read, may seem "inconsistent," one must know the whole counsel of God's Word to see there is no contradiction.

Q. What is the difference between the Old Testament and the New Testament?

A. The purpose of the Old Testament is to show us man's creation, his sin (fall), and to show us God's preparation for a Redeemer to come Who would make salvation available to all men. This Redeemer (Jesus) came through the Jewish nation; thus the Old Testament is the story of their history—good and bad.

In the New Testament we have the manifestation of the Redeemer and His manifestation through His people (those who receive Him). We also see the culmination of God's plan of redemption in the book of Revelation.

Q. Which version of the Bible do you believe is the most accurate?

A. From the time that God confused language at the tower of Babel until now, the human race has been trying to communicate through the imperfect vehicle of foreign languages. The Bible was written in Hebrew, Aramaic, and Greek. Because different words can be translated in a variety of ways, we have different Bible versions, which essentially are different translations.

Modern translations are taken from the original Greek and Hebrew; but even so, there is still a problem in that one word can have various shades and meanings and thereby can be translated differently. So each person who translates a work must do it on the basis of the context in which the word is written in order to determine the original meaning. Different scholars have different opinions on how these words should be translated; thus we have a variety of translations, and all of these translations depend upon the text from which that particular language was translated.

The NEW AMERICAN STANDARD VERSION and the NEW INTERNATIONAL VERSION are considered by many Bible scholars to be the most accurate English translations available today. However, my personal preference is still the KING JAMES VERSION.

Q. What does it mean to walk with God every day? How can I walk with Him every day?

A. "To walk with God" means to live your life in harmony with Christ's life in you. This comes about through prayer and Bible study. Speak to God in prayer, and let Him speak to you through the Bible.

Q. Please explain what "rightly dividing the word of truth" (II Timothy 2:15) means.

A. The Bible says that no scripture is a matter of one's own interpretation, but that scripture is to be interpreted through the revelation of the Holy Spirit. "Rightly dividing the word of truth" refers to this and means to take the scriptures within the context they are given in order to interpret the scriptures. Not only are we to take scriptures within the context that they are given in the chapter but also within the context of the Old and New Testaments as well. You must take into consideration the full counsel of God in light of how Jesus revealed the Father to us while He was here on earth.

Q. Is it better to read the Bible out loud? I heard once that it is because faith comes by hearing the Word of God.

A. God gives everyone the same measure of faith according to Romans 12:3; so faith is simply a matter of choice—choosing to believe or not to believe. The way we increase our faith is by hearing the Word of God (Romans 10:17). So whenever your faith seems weak, go to the Word of God! Live in the Word; dwell in the Word; meditate on the Word. The Word of God is your spiritual food and makes your faith strong. It's hard work; but it produces faith, and faith produces results!

If we are to take the Word literally, then there is a definite advantage to reading the Word out loud and hearing it. A lot of times I play tapes of the Word of God, and this is helpful as I'm driving a car or involved in activities where I can listen. I believe you'll find it a great blessing. Try it and see!

Q. Please explain what happened during the years between Malachi and Matthew.

A. The years between the time of Malachi and Matthew were years in which Israel had no prophet. No new Words of God were communicated, and no prophets nor spokesmen were available to Israel. According to Jewish history, Israel was occupied and ruled by foreigners and there were several uprisings such as the Maccabean uprising—but for the most part these times of rebellion had little positive result. Also during this time the Roman Empire was expanding and eventually controlled much of the known world—including Israel. It was during the time of the Roman occupation of Israel that God raised up two intercessors—Anna and Simeon—who prayed that they might see the Redeemer. The answer to their prayers was manifested in Jesus. (See Luke 2:25-38.)

Q. How do we know Jesus is God?

A. The Bible, which is the final authority for every Christian, says in John 1:1,14, *"In the beginning was the Word, and the Word was with God, and the Word was God. And the Word was made flesh, and dwelt among us, ..."* Philippians 2:6,7 tells us, *"Who, being in the form of God, thought it not robbery to be equal with God. But made himself of no reputation, and took upon him the form of a servant, and was made in the likeness of men."* These verses refer to Jesus Christ. They tell us that Jesus is God Who became man and lived here on earth.

If Jesus is not God, then we, of all people—that is to say Christians—are the most to be pitied. If Jesus is not God, then we have no hope for eternal life because a mere man could not ascend into heaven and sit at the Father's right hand as the Scriptures record.

I would encourage you to ask the Holy Spirit to open up your eyes to the fact that Jesus Christ is true God and true man. Come before Him in prayer and ask Him to reveal Himself to you in a personal way. If you are honestly seeking for the truth, then I know that He will do this for you.

Q. Marilyn, please explain the Trinity. If Jesus is God and the Holy Spirit is God and God the Father is God, how can Jesus sit at the right hand of Himself?

A. The concept of the Trinity (three-in-one and one-in-three) is ultimately a mystery to our human, finite minds! I can only tell you what I understand about it as I read through the Bible. Ultimately the truth about the Godhead must be accepted by faith so long as we are in these human bodies.

Although the word "trinity" is never mentioned in the Bible, its existence is clearly spoken of in Matthew 28:19 and II Corinthians 13:14. God is one (Deuteronomy 6:4), yet made up of three distinct persons: the Father, the Son, and the Holy Spirit.

Just as a family is *one* unit made up of several family members, so the Godhead is *one* unit with three members. Each person of the Trinity has a specific role, differing from the other two; and yet together, they make up a single unit with a single purpose, carrying out a perfect and complete plan.

The Heavenly Father is the architect or planner of the Trinity; Jesus is the contractor or the One Who carries out the plan; and the Holy Spirit is the laborer or the One Who gives life to the plan. Let's look at the creation record. The Father planned it, Jesus did it, and the Holy Spirit gave it life. These three distinct roles, or ministries, of the Trinity can be seen in the creation of man and the birth and resurrection of Jesus in the flesh. (See Genesis 1:2; 1:26; and John 1:2.)

The Old Testament scriptures which refer to God as one God, literally mean that He is a unit, not that He is only one individual. When you see this relationship, you can understand that Jesus the Son can sit at the right-hand of the Father.

Q. What does the name "Jehovah" mean? Who is Jehovah—God the Father or the Lord Jesus Christ?

A. The name *Jehovah* is the European pronunciation of an unspoken Hebrew name of God. It derives from the Hebrew tetragram (a four-letter word) *Yhvh*. This sacred name comes from the Hebrew verb *Havah* which means *"to be, or being"*; the implication of its meaning then is "God Who always was, still is, and always will be." Whether you are concerned about your past, your present, or your future, God has revealed ALL of Himself to meet your every need.

Jehovah is Jesus. For every revelation that Jehovah gave of Himself in the Old Testament, Jesus declared Himself to have that same quality or name in the New Testament. For example, Jehovah said to Moses, *"I AM WHO I AM"* (Exodus 3:14). Jesus identified Himself as "I am the Alpha and Omega, the beginning and the end" in Revelation. Jesus said, ". . . *before Abraham was,*

I am'' (John 8:58). The Jews knew that Jesus was claiming to be Jehovah God, and they picked up stones to throw at Him!

Q. Please explain for me, Marilyn, what is the grace of God?

A. ''Grace'' comes from the Hebrew word *chanan* which means ''to stoop in kindness to an inferior.'' The grace of God conveys that same idea in that we receive unmerited, unearned, undeserved favor from God. God's gifts are based on His undying mercies not on some kind of reward system for our works. God's kindness is not only present in Him in great measure but is manifest to us in abundance.

One of the best ways to remember what grace means is in an acrostic made of each letter in the word GRACE—''**G**od's **R**iches **A**t **C**hrist's **E**xpense.'' Without Christ's sacrifice none of us could receive God's grace.

Take the gift of grace today; and as you receive from Him that grace, give it away also that you may be ever abounding in His never ending grace (Romans 5:15-21).

Q. What is the meaning of the ''fear of the Lord?''

A. The word *fear* comes from a Hebrew root word which means ''to reverence, trust, and stand in awe.'' So this word is talking about the deep reverence and awe we should have for God. It is in this same trust, awe, and reverence that we should worship, love, and honor God.

Q. Why did God get so angry in Deuteronomy 32:19-22?

A. This passage of scripture records Israel's fall into idolatry. Idolatry is a turning away from the true and living God Who created us for fellowship. It is a sin in which the created is worshiped rather than the Creator (Romans 1:25). The sin of idolatry is so grievous to God because it separates us from Him, opens doors to Satan, and sends a person without Christ to hell.

First Samuel 15:23 also links idolatry with the sin of rebellion: *"For rebellion is as the sin of witchcraft, and stubbornness is as iniquity and idolatry . . . ."* Rebellion is the one state in a person's heart with which God cannot deal. He can deal with foolishness, ignorance, and even sin if a person is seeking God with his heart. But if a person has chosen to turn away in rebellion by an act of his will, God will not violate that free will.

In the Hebrew this word *anger* actually means "vexed, bitter, grieved, or sorrowful." So we could very accurately say that idolatry grieves God or causes him sorrow; that would be a better understanding of the original text.

Q. Has God terminated His plan or purpose for the Jews?

A. God has not ended His plan or purpose for the Jews. Paul said that their temporary blindness is for the purpose of Gentile salvation (Romans 11:25). At the time of the "fullness of the Gentiles," God will once again take up His plan for the Jews.

I would suggest you read and study Romans 10 and 11 for a clearer understanding of God's remnant. A good study Bible, such as DAKE'S ANNOTATED REFERENCE BIBLE, would provide you with many cross references and explanations concerning this topic. God bless your diligent study of His Word!

Chapter Two

SALVATION AND BAPTISM

Q. So many people say that salvation requires just confessing, believing, and obeying—and is open to all who ask for it. But, Marilyn, what about the scripture that says, "narrow is the way?"

A. Matthew 7:14 says, *"Because strait is the gate, and narrow is the way, which leadeth unto life, and few there be that find it."* In this scripture Jesus was referring to Himself as the "gate." He said later, ". . . *I am the way, the truth, and the life: no man cometh unto the Father, but by me"* (John 14:6). In other words, the way to salvation is narrow because salvation does not come through Buddha, Mohammed, good works, or any other means, except Jesus alone. He is the only way to salvation; when we come to salvation through Him, we only need to believe in our heart that God raised Jesus from the dead, confess Jesus as Lord, and we will be saved. (See Romans 10:9,10.)

Q. What does it mean to work out your own salvation?

A. Philippians 2:12,13 are very encouraging passages. They tell us that we are perfect vessels through which God can work and do His will. Paul exhorts the Christians to daily live out or experience their salvation. Our salvation is a practical thing; and we should always put our deliverance, redemption, and healing (that is salvation) into practice (Romans 1:16,17; 10:10). "With fear and trembling," is a strong admonition to beware of falling back into the flesh to accomplish Christ's will for our lives (John 6:63).

Q. I've been baptized in Jesus' name. Though I pray daily, I don't read the Bible daily and I don't attend church weekly. When I die will I go to heaven or hell?

A. Being baptized does not assure one's salvation. Even reading the Bible daily and going to church regularly do not assure you of a place in heaven. There is only one way to avoid hell and go to heaven. Jesus said that we must be "born again" to enter the kingdom of God (see John 3:5-8). If you have not been "born again," you will go to hell.

But I have good news for you! The Bible also tells us how we can be born again. To be born again, you must receive Jesus as your personal Lord and Savior: "*. . . if thou shalt confess with thy mouth the Lord Jesus, and shalt believe in thine heart that God hath raised him from the dead, thou shalt be saved. For with the heart man believeth unto righteousness; and with the mouth confession is made unto salvation*" (Romans 10:9,10). If you have not made such a confession but have a desire to do this, simply pray this prayer sincerely:

"Dear Jesus, I believe that You died for me and that You rose again on the third day. I confess to You that I am a sinner and that I need Your love and forgiveness. Come into my life, forgive my sins, and give me eternal life. I believe that God has raised You from the dead, and I now confess You as my Lord. Thank You for causing me to be born again!"

If you have received Jesus as your personal Savior, I want to encourage you to find a Spirit-filled church that can help you grow in the things of the Lord.

Q. Marilyn, I have heard you talk about man being a "triune" being and that Jesus redeems the "whole" man. Can you explain what you mean by this?

A. In I Thessalonians 5:23 we are told: *"And the very God of peace sanctify you wholly; and I pray God your whole spirit and soul and body be preserved blameless unto the coming of our Lord Jesus Christ."*

There it is! Man is a triune or three-part being who is made up of a spirit, a soul, and a body. Your spirit is your "new" or "regenerated" man. When you made Christ your Savior, your new spirit was given life by the Holy Spirit.

Your soul is made up of your mind, your emotions, and your will; our souls must be submitted to our spirits because the soul area is the place where decisions are made. As Christians we can rely on God for wisdom with which to make those decisions: "*If any of you lack wisdom, let him ask of God, . . .* " (James 1:5). The wisdom of this world appeals to our mind and emotions, but it tends to "puff up," rather than "build up." But when—by our wills—we put God's Word first, then we begin conforming our souls to the likeness of Jesus.

Some Christians live "soulishly," not discerning spiritual things. But you can have spiritual understanding: "*For the Word of God is quick, and powerful, and sharper than any twoedged sword, piercing even to the dividing asunder of soul and spirit, and of the joints and marrow, and is a discerner of the thoughts and intents of the heart*" (Hebrews 4:12). God's Word removes soulish thinking. For that reason, Christians should never go one day without reading God's Word. If we want to be conformed to Jesus' image, we must take in His knowledge through our spirits.

God's plan of redemption—belief in Jesus Christ and His work on the Cross—covers every area of your being and redeems the "whole" man. A Christian whose soul is directed by God's Word is a spiritual Christian. He is not his own authority because God is his authority. Your spirit is the "candle of the Lord." He will illuminate all that you do!

Q. My husband and I are retired, and we finally found Jesus just a few years ago. How could I go to church and teach Sunday school without being born again? or sing the "Hallelujah" chorus for twenty years without being born again?

A. Many, many people have been involved in church activities of all kinds but have not been born again. They have a head knowledge of the Lord, but not heart knowledge. However, as with you, there comes a time when the Holy Spirit illuminates their hearts to see that they really haven't had a born-again experience and they need to receive Jesus as Lord and Savior. At that time they become born again.

Q. Marilyn, I've heard you talk about the process of sanctification. Can you explain what you mean?

A. To ''sanctify'' means ''to be set apart.'' Every believer needs to be set apart from the world's system of thinking and acting. Jesus said to His disciples: *''Now ye are clean [sanctified] through the word which I have spoken unto you''* (John 15:3). So in answer to your question, sanctification is a process of being made holy. Yes, we are sanctified when we are born again; but the sanctification process continues when we read the Word and are led into a holy life by the Holy Spirit.

Q. Years ago I had an anointing of the Lord, but I backslid. Since then I have rededicated my life to the Lord, but I don't have the peace and joy of the Lord that I once had. What do you suggest I do?

A. Let me begin by reassuring you that God does love the backslider. The Lord is ever watching and desires to draw backslidden people back by the power of the Holy Spirit.

The first thing I suggest you do is to have a talk with your heart, according to I John 3:20,21: *''For if our heart condemn us, God is greater than our heart, and knoweth all things. Beloved, if our heart condemn us not, then have we confidence toward God.''* Tell your heart to quit condemning you! According to I John 1:9 when you confessed your sins and repented of them, then God was faithful and just to forgive you and cleanse you from all unrighteousness. Since you have already been forgiven, you do not need to repent a second time.

When Christians tell me that their relationship with the Lord has changed, I like to respond with the fact that the Lord hasn't moved, so they must have. I would suggest that you think back to all the things you were doing when you first became a Christian. Ask the Lord to reveal to you if there is an area of your life where you are doing something different than you did when you had peace and joy. Then return to doing that very thing.

Another thing that can rob you of peace and joy is murmuring. This will cause hardness in your heart and an inability to receive joy from the Lord. I believe that as you offer up a sacrifice of praise unto God, your soul will respond and begin to rejoice. Praise must be an act of the will, not done from emotions—or when you FEEL like it. As you develop a habit of praise, your peace and your joy will certainly return.

Q. I have several questions regarding baptism. If you've been baptized, are you saved? Should Christians be water baptized? What is the correct way to baptize—by sprinkling or immersion? What does the Bible say about it?

A. Water baptism does not save the soul. The thief on the Cross next to Jesus was not water baptized. Yet Jesus told the thief, "Today you will be with me in Paradise." The man's soul was saved without water baptism. Take assurance in the Lord's own words that water baptism in itself does not save a person's soul. Jesus said that we must be born again to enter the kingdom of God.

I do believe that water baptism should follow a person's decision for Jesus. Baptism is a wonderful statement to the world that testifies, "I'm a new creature in Christ. Now I am being baptized in obedience to God's Word." Often water baptism is a new Christian's first act of obedience to the Father! This becomes a public announcement that the person being baptized has now become a part of the family of God (Acts 8:26-38; I Peter 3:21).

Jesus was baptized (Luke 3:21-23), and He encouraged others to do so as well (see Luke 7:29,30); He even told His followers to baptize other people (Matthew 28:19).

Regarding the question of whether to sprinkle or immerse, you will find your answer has been lost in translation. The word *baptize* was transliterated—rather than translated—from the word *baptizo*, meaning ''to immerse.'' Jesus was immersed in water at His baptism; Matthew 3:16 speaks of the Lord coming ''up out of'' the water.

Q. Should a baby be baptized, or should a parent wait until the child is old enough to make his/her own decision?

A. First of all, I believe that infant baptism has been incorporated into the Church as a sincere act of dedication. However, the Bible says that repentance must accompany baptism. A baby has not sinned, nor can he repent; so he doesn't need to be baptized. Dedication of the child by his parents can be done, but nobody can make another person's decision to be saved.

Q. When I was 15, I joined the church and was baptized. But I never really lived for Jesus and really didn't know about the indwelling Christ. Ten years later I really repented and asked Jesus to come and dwell in my heart, and I continue to live for Him. According to the Bible, do I need to be baptized again?

A. If someone is truly born again and baptized and then backslides, he or she does not need to be baptized a second time when they return to the Lord, although the Scriptures do not expressly forbid such a practice. Water baptism is an outward symbol of the inward reality of our entrance into the Body of Christ, which only happens once (I Corinthians 12:13).

Q. I have read that when we receive Christ, we are baptized in the Holy Spirit. Is this different from being baptized in water?

A. Actually, you are speaking of three distinct things: receiving

Christ means you will live eternally with Him in heaven. Being baptized in the Holy Spirit is an empowering of the Holy Spirit. It is spoken of in Acts 2:4 when Christ told His disciples to wait on the empowering of the Holy Spirit before going out to witness. Water baptism is an act of an outward statement to the world of a spiritual happening that you are shedding sin and are washed clean in Jesus.

Q. Please explain the baptism of fire.

A. John the Baptist often spoke of being baptized with the Holy Spirit and with fire: *"I indeed baptize you with water unto repentance: but he that cometh after me is mightier than I, whose shoes I am not worthy to bear: he shall baptize you with the Holy Ghost, and with fire"* (Matthew 3:11).

The word in the Greek for fire literally means "fire" or "purging." I believe that when John the Baptist spoke of a baptism of fire, he was referring to the refining that the Holy Spirit will do in our lives once we receive the baptism of the Spirit.

God is continually calling us to holiness and cleanliness from sin. He is "burning" the dross in our lives to refine us as gold. Sometimes God's discipline and cleansing can be painful, but it doesn't have to be. Jesus said in John 15:3, *"Now ye are clean through the word which I have spoken unto you."* Jesus was saying we can be purged through the words which He has spoken to us. It is the Word that washes us; it is the Word that cleanses us; and it is the Word that purifies us as if by fire.

Q. John 4:2 says that Jesus Himself did not baptize. Why not?

A. I'm not sure why Jesus didn't baptize, but I think He may purposely have refrained from this activity so that we would see that baptism has nothing to do with our salvation. Baptism is an outward expression of the inward transaction of salvation. Too much emphasis would probably have been placed upon baptism if Jesus had baptized, or jealousy might have arisen between those baptized by Jesus and those who were not. Paul addressed this problem in I Corinthians!

Chapter Three

THE CHURCH AND THE HOLY SPIRIT

Q. If God told the Israelites to observe the Sabbath on the seventh day, why do we observe the Sabbath on Sunday?

A. Most people think that *Sabbath* means "the day we go to church and worship." The word *Sabbath* comes from the Hebrew word for "rest." The Jews rested on the seventh day as God commanded; however, the day on which Sabbath occurs is not important. Rather, the important thing is the cessation of work to rest in God.

After Jesus' resurrection, the early Christian Church gathered on Sundays to celebrate the Resurrection which occurred on that day of the week. Since that time it has been the custom of Christians to celebrate every Sunday in commemoration of the Resurrection.

In Mark 2:27 Jesus said "*. . . The sabbath was made for man, and not man for the sabbath.*" Hebrews 4:9,10 says that our rest is the ceasing from works to please God by entering into grace. For Christians, every day can be a sabbath because God has given us His eternal grace that is all-sufficient.

Q. When I gave my life to Jesus, I thought I joined the Body of Christ. Is it scriptural for people to join a church and go through membership class?

A. I agree that you joined the Body of Christ when you became a believer. However, the book of Hebrews says not to forsake the assembling of believers. I personally believe that there is a corporate anointing and protection that is imparted to everyone who commits to membership in a local body. Church membership also gives you an opportunity to work for the Lord in His body.

Church membership is not taught in Scripture, but much is said—especially in Paul's letters—about the local fellowship of believers. They were obviously a close-knit family, led by a pastor from whom they received spiritual teaching, leadership, and counsel.

Membership classes are intended to build one's spiritual foundation, and to assure a person of salvation according to the Word. Every believer should know basic Christian doctrine and how to prove it in the Word. I believe that membership classes are an act of love toward members. Most churches that hold membership classes do it because they love their people and want to make sure that they have the basic foundations of the Word.

The books of Timothy and Titus deal specifically with church leadership and church order in the local fellowship. Second Peter deals with heresy in the church, and nearly all of Paul's letters are written to local bodies of believers. So this is a very important subject to God.

Q. Marilyn, why is it necessary to go to church? I watch a lot of Christian shows on TV (including yours) and listen to Christian radio, and they really minister to me.

A. The scriptural reasons for going to church are found in Hebrews 10:25: "*Not forsaking the assembling of ourselves together, as the manner of some is; but exhorting one another: and so much the more, as ye see the day approaching.*" You cannot "assemble together" through the television and radio, although these are excellent teaching and evangelistic tools. We are also told in Ephesians 4:11-13 that pastors and other ministers are given to build up the Body of Christ and cause it to come into maturity. Every Christian needs the personal ministry, love, and encouragement that the local Body can give.

Q. I am in a denominational church even though I am born again and Spirit filled. I really love many of the people there but feel that I am missing out on something since it is not charismatic.

Should I find another church or stay where I am?

A. I would advise you to earnestly seek the Lord for an answer to your question. If you are led to stay in the church where you are, then perhaps you can attend their main service, which is probably on Sunday mornings. Go to that service, pray, and be a light to those people. Be loving, walk in God's wisdom, speak words of faith, and intercede for the pastor.

Then find a Spirit-filled church that can really feed you, and go on Sunday and Wednesday evenings. Get involved with Spirit-filled friends and prayer meetings. Our own church has many such people who attend two churches. We call them "moonlighters"—they "moonlight" with us in the evenings, but on Sunday mornings they are a great blessing to another church. This other church has become like a missions program for them. And in the meantime, we are happy to supply their "spiritual food" and ammunition to be warriors and lights in dark areas.

On the other hand, if you are unable to let your light and testimony of the Holy Spirit be known in that church, I question that it is God's will for you to remain. If this local body is not sound in Christian doctrine, then you may be in a "liberal" church controlled by a hierarchy rather than the Spirit of God. If you are certain of its liberalism, you should give your tithes into a church where you are fed.

It is important for you to pray for the liberals, bind Satan, command the blindness to come from their eyes, and believe for revival among them—or that the liberals be removed. I doubt that a personal rebuke would help in this situation, but you can rebuke Satan. Another option is for you to write to the leadership and express your views.

Q. I'm leery and suspicious about what kind of church to attend. Can you give me some guidance in this area?

A. You will never find a perfect church; so my basic advice would be to find a church which preaches the whole gospel and does not compromise in any area regarding the Word of God. If the Word of God is taught in its fullness, then that church will be blessed by the Lord and will bless you. The best plumb line to use in measuring whether a church is "right on" or not is to ask yourself this question: "Does the teaching, preaching, and practice of this church line up with the Word of God?" If so, the church is a true church of Jesus Christ; if not, avoid it.

I would encourage you to visit several churches and let the Holy Spirit witness to your heart about whether or not they are of the Lord.

Q. I hear a lot about submission to a pastor, but to what extent? I desire God's will in every area, including this.

A. Submit does not, of course, mean to be in slavery. It is a military word which means "to get in marching order." You should submit to your pastor, husband, or other authority as long as they are giving counsel out of God's Word. If they give you counsel against God's Word, then you are not obligated to submit. I would simply encourage you to be sure that you do not have a rebellious heart and that your biggest desire is to build the kingdom.

Q. What's the difference between a pastor and a minister?

A. A pastor, one of the five-fold ministry gifts (Ephesians 4:11), is in charge of a church congregation. The pastor's responsibility is to feed the flock with the Word of God, to watch over them in spiritual matters, and to nurture them into a place of maturity.

The word *minister* is a more generic term which can include any of the five-fold gifts such as apostle, pastor, prophet, evangelist, or teacher. Anyone in one of these offices is referred to as a "minister." So, all pastors are ministers, but not all ministers are pastors! In addition, anyone in the Body of Christ can be a "minister," in the sense that they minister to one another and to the Lord. Ministry is simply a term of service within the Body of Christ.

Q. Marilyn, please explain the "priesthood of the believer."

A. The priests of the Old Testament were representatives for the people in the offering of sacrifices and service to God. These priests were consecrated unto the work of the Lord (Exodus 29:29-37). Today, all members of the Body of Christ are said to be priests (I Peter 2:5,9). Basically this means that we each have the right to approach God and offer sacrifices and service to Him (Hebrews 13:15).

Q. Do you believe there are prophets and apostles living today? If so, please give scripture concerning this. Also, can you tell me why some churches, as a whole, do not have a recognized office of an apostle or prophet?

A. The ministry of the apostle and prophet is little understood, and even less recognized in most denominational churches. Nonetheless, apostles and prophets are as valid today as are evangelists, pastors, and teachers. They are necessary in order for the Body of Christ to come into unity. That is why the devil is fighting the ministry gifts of apostle and prophet so desperately.

When Jesus ascended, He gave us the five-fold ministry gifts to equip the saints and to build up the Body of Christ. These are listed in Ephesians 4:11,12 (NAS): " . . . *He gave some as apostles, and some as prophets, and some as evangelists, and some as pastors and teachers, for the equipping of the saints for the work of the service, to the building up of the body of Christ.*" Verse 13 goes on to tell us that these gifts are to remain until we all attain to the "unity of the faith," and mature in the Lord.

I believe a time is coming very soon when we will see this type of unity flourish in the Body of Christ, and we will no longer act like children carried about by every wind of doctrine. The time is soon to come when the Church is going to grow up as one Body fitted and held together in love.

I would encourage you to study and meditate on the fourth chapter of Ephesians in order to understand more fully these ministry gifts.

Q. My question concerns prophets. Can a prophet of God ever give a false prophecy? How do we recognize false prophets? When someone begins to function in the gifts of the Spirit, is there any room for "practice"?

A. First of all let me clarify something: there is a big difference between the prophet's ministry and the gift of prophecy. The gift of prophecy is one of the nine gifts listed in I Corinthians 12 and may be exercised by any member of Christ's Body under the unction of the Holy Spirit.

The prophet's ministry is a full-time ministry; according to the Scriptures, the prophet is judged by whether his/her words come to pass. If they do not, the individual is a false prophet. However, each person called to this ministry grows and develops in that calling, and no one in the flesh is perfect; but when a person steps out into the full-time ministry of a prophet, then his words should always come to pass.

False prophets have several distinct characteristics: (1) they will not submit to the leadership of the local church; (2) they usually give "words" that are harsh and judgmental—often to their own benefit, such as, "The Lord says to sell your car and give me the money"; (3) they want a following of people, and they exalt the flesh by pointing to themselves or to their "gifts"; and (4) they cause strife, confusion, and division in local bodies, and leave a destructive path of crippled, hurting sheep wherever they go. Paul warned of these, and called them grievous wolves (Acts 20:29).

I believe that God does give us room for making mistakes, and that we do need to practice our gift. At one time or another, we have all gotten into the flesh and "missed it." The key to keeping the flesh out of the way is to stay in the Word and walk in the Spirit. As we grow in knowledge and understanding of the Word, the "Words from the Lord"—or this gift of prophecy working through us to the edification of the Body—will become more and more accurate as we learn to discern the difference between the voice of God and the voice of the flesh.

Q. Was the witch of Endor really able to conjure up the spirit of Samuel?

A. For every spiritual gift that God has, Satan has a counterfeit. The spirit which prophesied to Saul was indeed a counterfeit spirit. First Chronicles 10:13,14 verifies the fact that it was a familiar spirit who prophesied Satan's plan to Saul.

As Christians, we must be very wise and discerning in every prophecy that we receive. Not everything that is prophesied is necessarily from God. First John 1:4 tells us to test the spirits to see whether they are of God, and we are wise to heed this warning.

Q. I've heard a lot of talk about "the anointing." What is the anointing? Do all preachers and teachers have it? Does it come and go? Are all messages anointed—or should they be?

A. There are different types of anointings, but all believers should have the basic anointing of the Holy Spirit. Acts 1:8 tells us about this general anointing: "*But ye shall receive power, after that the Holy Ghost is come upon you: . . . .*" The baptism of the Holy Spirit is a general anointing, which is an endowment of power to do the works that Jesus did.

There are also special anointings which the Holy Spirit endows upon the five-fold ministry gifts. The anointing for a ministry does not come and go if the people who are operating in the ministry gifts have been truly called and appointed by the Lord (see Ephesians 4).

Not all messages given by the five-fold ministry are necessarily anointed. Even people in the ministry can get into the flesh at times; but that is not for us to judge, nor does it mean that the anointing has left them. The anointing also teaches you about all things (see I John 2:27).

Finally, the I Corinthians 12 gifts, which are the manifestation gifts of the Holy Spirit, operate under an anointing which is according to the moving of the Holy Spirit for a specific occasion.

Q. How can I receive the baptism in the Holy Spirit?

A. Acts 1:8 promises you: *"But ye shall receive power, after that the Holy Ghost is come upon you . . . ."* Then Luke 11:13 assures you with: *". . . how much more shall your heavenly Father give the Holy Spirit to them that ask him?"* The Word tells you that when you ask, be ready to receive. Tell God that you do receive His gift. Thank Him for the baptism of the Holy Spirit, and believe His Word.

Once you believe that you receive, then by faith begin to speak out loud in syllables and sounds that are not English. This will sound strange to your mind, and your mind may think, "This can't be the Holy Spirit!" But Romans 8:7 tells us that our fleshly mind opposes the things of God. If this happens, simply make the decision to trust the Word. Acts 2:4 tell us, *"And they were all filled with the Holy Ghost, and began to speak with other tongues, as the Spirit gave them utterance."*

Q. Is the gift of tongues scriptural? Would you please give me some scripture references?

A. Yes, the gift of tongues is scriptural: it is found in Acts 2:4 and in I Corinthians 12-14—and is most certainly of God. As you read the book of Acts, you will see many instances and references to the operation of this important gift from God.

First Corinthians 14 even provides us with a scriptural order in operating in the gifts of the Spirit. When a *message* in tongues is given to the Church, an *interpretation* must also be given. It is possible that several people can receive the interpretation for the message in tongues; but in order to eliminate confusion, only one and at the most two people are to give an interpretation for that tongue. Verse 39 even says: "*. . . forbid not to speak with tongues.*" Singing in the Spirit is a beautiful act of corporate worship, as long as the body of believers is submitted to the worship leader and not causing confusion by "doing their own thing."

Q. Marilyn, What exactly is praying in tongues? If tongues is a real language as spoken of in Acts, why do people who minister overseas have to have an interpreter to translate? Is there a difference in the "prayer language" in the book of Acts and "tongues" in I Corinthians 14?

A. When we pray in tongues, the Holy Spirit prays through us (Romans 8:26,27). What may at first seem like "mumbo-jumbo" is in reality a heavenly language which neither our earthly minds nor Satan can understand. In my own experience, however, the more you pray in tongues, the more you can begin to recognize certain phrases and sounds. Sometimes, I ask for an interpretation and God tells me through my spirit what I am praying.

I have also received reports from many missionaries who have gone to foreign lands, have preached in tongues, and the people have understood. So tongues is as valid today as it was in Acts 2:6, but it is as the Holy Spirit directs. God can use tongues, but He can also use an interpreter.

There is a difference between tongues and a prayer language. A prayer language is personal, direct intercession/petition/

communication to the Father from the Holy Spirit within us. This builds or edifies us personally (Jude 20).

A public tongue must be interpreted and accompanied with a supernatural interpretation. This is the equivalent of prophecy (I Corinthians 14:5).

Q. I am a born-again believer and know that I am filled with the Holy Spirit, but I do not speak in tongues. My question is, can you be Spirit-filled and not speak in tongues?

A. The answer to your question is found in Mark 16:17: *"And these signs shall follow them that believe; . . . they shall speak with new tongues."* It's very clear here that the signs that He lists in these verses *will* accompany those who believe. The scriptural pattern in the book of Acts beginning with the 120 in the upper room is that those who received the baptism of the Holy Spirit manifested it with the evidence of tongues. This, however, does not necessarily mean that you are not Spirit-filled.

I have met several people who by faith received the baptism of the Holy Spirit and later manifested tongues. But I believe that tongues will always be manifested in those who are baptized in the Holy Spirit, if they are open to all God has for them. Speech is a mechanical operation used either by our mind or spirit. Most people when properly instructed on how to yield the instruments of speech will receive their language.

Q. How can I find out what I am saying in tongues?

A. Many of the early Christians must have asked this question as well, because Paul made sure he addressed this point in his first letter to the Corinthians: *"For if I pray in an unknown tongue, my spirit prayeth, but my understanding is unfruitful"* (I Corinthians 14:14).

The Bible tells you that your spirit knows what you are saying, but your mind does not. So the only way you can find out what you are praying by the Spirit is to ask the Lord to give you revelation so you can interpret what you are praying. Nonetheless, I have found that it is important not to get caught up in trying to figure out what I am saying, but it is important to be consistent in prayer and to trust the Holy Spirit to pray that perfect prayer through me.

Sometimes I will pray with the Spirit and then I will be impressed of the Lord to interpret what I have said. In this way I find out what the Holy Spirit has been praying through me and my understanding then is enlightened. Another place in Scripture says we speak mysteries, but I Corinthians 2 tells us that the Spirit reveals these mysteries as we pray in the Spirit. So claim His promise to show you by revelation what you are speaking.

Q. Must I first confess my sins and repent before I use my prayer language?

A. When we pray in the Spirit (tongues), we have immediate access to the throne of God. The Holy Spirit Himself is praying through us as we pray in the Spirit, and there is no sin in the Holy Spirit.

In times of emergency, the very *first* thing we should do is pray in the Spirit. Romans 8:26,27 says: *"Likewise, the Spirit also helpeth our infirmities: for we know not what we should pray for as we ought: but the Spirit itself maketh intercession for us with groanings which cannot be uttered. And he that searcheth the heart knoweth what is the mind of the Spirit, because he maketh intercession for the saints according to the will of God."* The Holy Spirit knows our weaknesses and our infirmities, so He makes intercession for us through our prayer language. He prays a perfect prayer, and God hears His own Spirit as quickly as you hear your own voice when you speak.

It is also important for you to understand that because you have become righteous through Jesus Christ, you stand in a place before the Father through Jesus. Certainly there is a time and a place for us to confess our sins, but this is only necessary as the Holy Spirit convicts us of our sins.

Q. How can I grow from devotional tongues to the gift of diverse tongues?

A. Your devotional tongue was given to you when you were baptized in the Holy Spirit. It is a part of your prayer life and can be used at your will. However, the gift of diverse tongues is an operation of the Holy Spirit through an individual—and may be used only as the Holy Spirit wills. This gift is for the edification of the Body and must be accompanied with the gift of interpretation.

Q. I love the way you explain things, Marilyn, so I hope you can explain the difference between the gifts of the Holy Spirit in Romans 12 and the gifts in I Corinthians 12.

A. There are basically three types of gifts listed in the scriptures: the Romans 12 "motivational gifts," the I Corinthians 12 "manifestations of the Spirit," and the Ephesians 4 "ministry gifts."

Every born-again believer in the Body of Christ has a Romans 12 gift—a motivational gift. That gift motivates him to minister in a particular function such as giving. The gifts of the Spirit (I Corinthians 12) are given by the Spirit to manifest the work of the Lord Jesus Christ and to aid the Body of Christ. Generally speaking, those who have received the baptism of the Holy Spirit operate in the manifestation gifts. We are also told in Ephesians 4:11-13 that the ministry gifts are given to build up the Body of Christ and cause it to come into maturity.

Chapter Four
ANGELS AND DEMONS

Q. Are angels real? If they are, what are they like?

A. The Bible says that angels are just as real as you and I. They are a race of superb beings with an important mission—to carry out the will of God on the earth and to minister to mankind according to God's Word. They have a prominent place in Scripture, being mentioned over 300 times! We know from the Bible that God created the angels (Psalms 148:2,5) and that angels were present at the creation of the earth (Job 38:4,7).

We also know that there are ranks of angels including elect angels (I Timothy 5:21), the seraphim (Isaiah 6:1-3), the cherubim (Genesis 3:24), archangels (Jude 9), and guardian angels (Hebrews 1:14). We also know that a third of the angels fell with Lucifer (Revelation 12:3,4); these fallen angels (Satan and his followers) also have ranks.

Angels are not babies with wings. Angels eat, talk, hear what you say, and walk—and they move faster than the speed of light! Though in many ways they resemble man, they are what we would probably call super-human; they are not "better" than we are nor in any way "better" than God. Angels are mighty warriors who are very much involved with the works of God.

Q. A very close relative recently died. As a child I was told that people become angels when they die. Is my relative now my guardian angel?

A. People who die *never* become angels. Angels were created before mankind, and their function is to serve God and mankind (see Hebrews 1:13,14; Daniel 8:16; and Luke 1:19). God created humanity to be His family and to fellowship with Him. Therefore, your loved one cannot become a guardian angel since angels are of a different order in Creation.

The Scriptures are very clear on what happens when a Christian dies. Second Corinthians 5:8 tells us that when we are absent from the body, we are present with the Lord. At the point of physical death, the Christian is immediately in the Lord's presence.

Q. How do we know if and when the angels are helping or ministering to us? How can I get them to work for me? I don't see any evidence of them working in my life.

A. We seldom know when angels are helping us, but Hebrews 1:14 assures us that they are. On occasion people have known, after a specific incident, that they were aided by an angel—usually by the angel's sudden disappearance. Hebrews 13:2 says that it is possible even to give hospitality to angels without knowing it.

As children of God we are automatically protected by an elite angelic force. The Bible says that the angel of the Lord *encamps* around those who fear God (Psalms 34:7). If you fear God (regard Him with deep love, respect, and awe), then you have an angelic encampment surrounding you.

It's one thing to know that there are thousands of angels who are ready and willing to minister to us and for us, and quite another thing to put them into action! If your angels aren't active, the only way to get them to move on your behalf—I call this "activating angels"—is through prayer. And don't pray just any old way. David said that angels move at the command of God's **Word** (Psalms 103:20). Praying God's Word unleashes His angels to perform the supernatural.

Q. On one of your TV shows you said that Jesus appeared on earth as an angel. Unfortunately, I was only half-listening at the time. Could you explain how this is possible? I believe that Jesus is God made man—not angel.

A. You are right. Jesus is God made man, the second person of the Trinity. What you must have heard was my teaching regarding "theophanies"—Old Testament appearances of Jesus on earth.

Many Bible commentators agree that Jesus sometimes came ''disguised'' as an *angel of the Lord* in the Old Testament. For example, ''the angel of the Lord'' appeared to Moses from out of the burning bush (Exodus 3:2). This angel was really God—an Old Testament manifestation of the Lord Jesus. The Dake's study Bible offers a fascinating study of times when ''the angel of the Lord'' refers to Jesus.

Q. I heard you say once that both the ''good'' and the ''bad'' angels influenced nations and leaders in the Bible. Do you think there are angelic forces seeking to influence government leaders today?

A. Angels are not only concerned with your personal affairs, they are also very much involved with the affairs of nations. Nowhere is this more clearly seen than in the book of Daniel. In Daniel 10 we are told about angelic warfare—*the prince of the kingdom of Persia* detained the angel Gabriel in a satanic blockade which prevented Daniel's prayers from being answered immediately.

I believe that high-ranking evil spirits are appointed over nations, and the prayers of God's people affect the outcome of those spirits' evil assignments. These few verses in Daniel give us insight into the powerful control such principalities and rulers of darkness may exercise over nations and national issues.

What's the easiest way to destroy a nation but to go after its leaders? Satan attempted to do this when he provoked King David (I Chronicles 21:1)—and he is still provoking national leaders and nations today. And just as in the days of David and Daniel, I believe the prayers of God's people greatly affect Satan's control over nations today. Those prayers enable God's angels to battle the evil principalities in charge of cities and nations.

That is why I so strongly urge believers to pray daily for their leaders at both the local and national levels and for their nations as a whole. Our prayers **can** and **do** influence our nations.

Q. Where do angels "fear to tread?"

A. The expression, "Fools rush in where angels fear to tread," is not in the Bible. You have ministering spirits—angels—who are sent on your behalf to perform the Word of God as you speak it from your lips. Although these angels may encounter Satan's fallen angels in carrying out their work (see Daniel 10:13), there is no indication from Scripture that they "fear" to work on our behalf. They will aid you in carrying out your authority based on God's Word (Hebrews 1:14).

Psalms 91:11 says: *"For he shall give his angels charge over thee, to keep thee in all thy ways."* It is the Father Who gives charge over the angels; so simply pray to the Father in the name of Jesus—ask Him to send His angels to do the specific work which you desire.

Q. In the beginning all the angels, including the devil, were in God's camp. Why is it then that when Christians see an angel from God it is beautiful but when they see the devil or one of his angels (demons), they are ugly?

A. Christians do not always see demons as ugly. It is a documented fact that many believers have seen demons as beautiful beings, which is the way they and Satan counterfeit themselves (see II Corinthians 11:14). Of course, when they are seen in their true character, they are hideously ugly and weak.

Q. Marilyn, are you implying through your book, SATAN-PROOF YOUR HOME, that Satan is omnipresent? I thought only God was.

A. I am in no way implying that Satan is omnipresent. Satan is not omnipresent, but he does have an army—an evil host of demons—who surround us. The Body of Christ needs to be informed of the presence of these wicked spiritual forces and to act upon them according to Ephesians 1,2, and 6.

Q. Marilyn, it says in the Bible that we should love our enemies. Am I supposed to love the devil?

A. At one time Satan was a very important and very beautiful angel named Lucifer, but he became so proud of himself that he decided he was better than God and thought he could be God. This terrible sin caused Lucifer to become Satan or the devil; and instead of being good, he became evil. Jesus told us to love our enemies; but we are never to love evil, and Satan is completely evil and wicked. God does not want us to love the devil or any of his ways (I Peter 3:11,12).

Q. I have always believed demons can oppress Christians, but do you believe demons can enter Christians?

A. I do not believe demons can enter Christians, but certain demons can affect Christians. They can oppress Christians, but a Christian cannot be demon possessed. The spirit of a Christian can't be overtaken by the devil; Christians can be oppressed in body, mind, emotions, and will, but not in spirit (John 8:32; Acts 10:38).

Q. Since demon spirits can possess human bodies, can angels also possess them?

A. Although angels are able to appear in human form at times (Genesis 18:2; Daniel 10:18; Zechariah 2:1), we never read of angels possessing humans in the Bible; instead, we are told that God's angels are sent to minister to those who will inherit salvation (Hebrews 1:14).

Q. I am concerned about a friend who is involved with a psychic. What can I DO to help her?

A. Your friend definitely needs a born-again experience with the Lord Jesus Christ. Her involvement with the psychic is absolutely against God's Word. Psychics get their information from demons and the devil. The Bible specifically warns against such practices and tells us to have nothing to do with those who use divination.

The very best advice I can give you on how to help is to be a gap stander. I encourage you to spend time praying in the Spirit. Perhaps you can even fast and pray. This breaks many yokes in other peoples' lives and strengthens your faith to believe. So the most effective action you can take is to pray, pray, pray!

Should the Lord give you an opportunity to present the gospel to your friend, perhaps you could start by explaining that we must be very careful to lead our lives according to the Word and not according to fortune telling or astrology. God's Word is our source of truth, and anything that does not line up with His Word is not from Him.

Palm reading, graph analysis, and other psychic practices are occult practices which Scripture condemns. Deuteronomy 18:10-12 says: "*There shall not be found among you any one . . . that useth divination, or an observer of times, or an enchanter, or a witch, Or a charmer, or a consulter with familiar spirits, or a wizard, or a necromancer. For all that do these things are an abomination unto the LORD . . . .*" In Exodus 22 the Lord commanded all those involved in witchcraft (mediums and anyone who practiced occult forms of religion) to be killed.

Q. Is there anything wrong with karate, kung-fu, and the other martial arts?

A. The phrase "martial arts" comes from the Greek god Mars, the "god of war." From this we know that any of the martial arts are strongly connected with spirits of violence, murder, and hatred, which are associated with war.

Karate, kung-fu, and other forms of martial arts are not just means of self-defense—they are actually a religion. Karate originates from an oriental religion which worships false gods and uses demonic power to perform violent acts—all cloaked in the disguise of self-defense.

Q. Please explain why manipulation is witchcraft.

A. One of the goals of witchcraft is to influence the behavior of others—to control them. Anytime we seek to control the free will of other individuals, we are practicing a form of witchcraft. Of course, this does not apply to parents who discipline and train their children or to other forms of behavior modification where the person is in agreement with the therapy offered by a counselor or other trained professionals. The key here is when someone wishes to selfishly control another person AGAINST their will. Sometimes this control starts out as subtle manipulation.

Q. I hear you and other well-known Bible teachers telling Christians to go out and do battle with the devil. Yet, Marilyn, I must confess that I am afraid to. I once was involved in the occult and know the power that I am supposed to come against, and I'm afraid of what it can do to me. Can you help me?

A. In Ephesians 1 and 2 we are told that Jesus is seated in heavenly places *far above* all demonic rulers and authorities; all of hell's forces are under His feet. That is wonderful; but even better yet, Ephesians 2:6 goes on to say that believers are seated *with Him* in heavenly places. That means demons and occult power are under OUR feet as well! As you meditate on these scriptures, the Word will produce faith and power in your heart to KNOW that demons must submit to your commands concerning them.

You also have ministering spirits—angels—who are sent on your behalf to perform the Word of God as you speak it from your lips. They will aid you in carrying out your authority based on God's Word.

So you see, there is never a reason for the believer to fear demonic power, but there is GREAT reason for demons to fear YOU when you discover and use the power you have in Jesus' name!

Q. Please tell me how I can speak confusion to the enemy.

A. There are many times in scripture where the enemy was confounded so that God's elect would know victory. (See Genesis 11:9; Exodus 14:24; Acts 21:31.) One good example is found in I Samuel 7:10—the Philistines were put to confusion as they came against Israel.

We can speak confusion to the enemy by standing on the evidence of the Word. God has caused the enemies' defeat in these examples so we know God can cause it to happen again. We can rest assured that because God loves us, He will do it for us. The enemy is confounded, and we are the victors!

Q. Can you bind evil spirits from entering or staying in your house, even if non-believers live with you?

A. As a believer you have the authority to bind evil spirits from entering into your house even if non-believers live with you. You have this authority over all evil influences. First Corinthians 7:14 tells us that one believing person can sanctify (make holy or clean) the whole household.

Q. Is there a way to quietly cast out demons without people knowing what is happening? Also, where are we supposed to send the demons that we cast out of someone?

A. Though it is possible to cast out demons without people knowing, it is not wise because the people being delivered need to have an opportunity to come to the knowledge of the truth. Then they can repent, and take authority over the demon itself—so it may not have the opportunity to re-enter. However, I have found that when discernment has been given by the Holy Spirit and I have received a Word from the Lord, this is the time to cast out a spirit. There does not need to be any disturbance whatsoever. You can simply take authority, command the spirits to be at peace, and leave.

When Jesus told us to take authority over Satan and cast him out, He gave no further instructions. The Word only says that they go and wander in "dry places" (Luke 11:24); and there is no scriptural admonition to "send them there." The only scriptural record of sending a spirit to a specific place is in Mark 5 where Jesus sent the demons into the pigs. Jesus may have wanted to prevent the demons from tearing the man and killing him as they left, since there were so many. We only need to be obedient to what Jesus told us, and that is to cast them out (Mark 16:17).

Chapter Five

HEARING FROM GOD AND KNOWING HIS WILL

Q. I'm not sure if I'm hearing God's voice or someone else's. What does God's voice sound like?

A. We all struggle with the question, "Is this the voice of God?" John 10 offers us a wonderful promise: The Lord's sheep know His voice, and the voice of a stranger they will not follow. The voice of God can come to us in different ways. In the Old Testament the voice of God is described as a still, small voice (I Kings 19:11,12). Most often God's voice sounds very much like our own thoughts. But these thoughts do not originate from the mind; they come from deep within our own spirit.

Believers have been promised that as we continue to walk with God, He will guide us with His eye upon us and lead us in the way that we should go (Psalms 32:8). And according to Galatians 5:16, we can know that we are being led by the Holy Spirit if we are walking in the Spirit; and walking in the Spirit means to act on God's Word, no matter what "sense-knowledge" tells us. I believe that our flesh seeks after signs—something we can see or feel. Check out the leadings you have by asking yourself, "Is this my flesh wanting a sign, or is this God's Word directing my spirit?" If you follow the Word, you will never be disappointed.

Q. Several people have told me that God has a special call on my life. Please help me find out what God's will is for my life.

A. I want to share with you three steps that have helped me discern the will of God for my life: (1) the desire must line up with the Word; (2) you should have an inner witness of your leading—the Holy Spirit bears witness with God's Word in your spirit which brings you peace; and (3) circumstances should line up accordingly. At times there may be a waiting period. The desire may be scriptural; you may have an inner witness; but circumstances may take some time before coming together. When this happens, it's important to be patient. It is never wise to try to make things come together on your own. God will bring to completion what He's begun (Proverbs 3:5,6).

You can trust God for your future. As you learn to rely more on Him and less on your own "feelings," you will find a peace that truly passes all understanding. Be very careful about accepting any "Word from the Lord" from others. Remember, all "words" must line up with *the* Word, your own inner witness, and the circumstances. Anytime we depend on someone else's understanding of God's will for our lives, we are putting ourselves in a place of danger.

Q. What do people mean when they talk about revelation knowledge?

A. God is continually giving us deeper revelation knowledge (insight) into His Word. However, the key to revelation knowledge is that it must always line up with and be tested according to the known Word of God—the Bible. Revealed knowledge often opens up God's Word to us in a fresh way—not adding to the Word nor taking away from it, but revealing it to us in a deeper way: *"But God hath revealed them unto us by his Spirit: for the Spirit searcheth all things, yea, the deep things of God"* (I Corinthians 2:10).

Jesus very clearly indicated to us that the Holy Spirit would be our teacher and teach us things by revelation (see John 14). I believe the apostle Paul was referring to revelation knowledge when he wrote about the revelation of mystery (Romans 16:25) and when he instructed the Corinthians in the use of spiritual gifts (I Corinthians 14:26). Paul also prayed that God would give the Church revelation in the knowledge of Him (Ephesians 1:17).

Nevertheless, Paul also warned that if any one, including an angel from heaven, came with a revelation other than the gospel which was brought to the world by Jesus, then we would know that revelation was not from God. So then any "revealed knowledge" beyond God's Word as found in the Bible is not of God. Nearly every cult has an additional source of written authority besides the Bible. These extra-Biblical scriptures are not from God.

Q. I think that God has called me to full-time ministry. Do you have a witness of my call? Where should I begin ministering?

A. There is nothing that delights my heart more than to see a believer called into full-time ministry. If you are truly called, it will be the number-one, consuming desire of your life and God will begin to open the doors for you. I cannot tell another person whether or not they are called, because God wants you to be certain in your own heart. It never hurts to "knock on doors" in order to find opportunities to minister. Be wise and discreet as you watch God open doors for you.

Also, I believe Bible school is a wise step in preparing for ministry. Second Timothy 2:15 tells us to, *"Study to shew thyself approved unto God, a workman that needeth not to be ashamed, ..."* I recommend my Bible college as a possibility for your training. We offer an Associate of Arts degree in Christian Education, Counseling, Pastoral Ministry, Youth Ministry, Missions, and General Ministry. The General Ministry Program is available either on-campus or through independent study by correspondence.

Q. I am struggling trying to keep the vision of my ministry. Have you ever been discouraged about serving God?

A. My heart has been deeply touched as I've traveled around the country and have met many individuals in the five-fold ministry asking similar questions. I do know how it feels to be discouraged, and at times I wondered whether I was really in God's will for my life and my ministry.

I want to encourage you not to give up hope. Please continue to press on to victory—it will come eventually as you trust in God's ability to deliver you from your circumstances.

God's Word promises that "*. . . lo, I am with you alway, even unto the end of the world*" (Matthew 28:20). Above all: "*. . . do not throw away your confidence, which has a great reward. For you have need of endurance, so that when you have done the will of God, you may receive what was promised*" (Hebrews 10:35,36 NAS).

Q. I'm resting now from near burnout from church duties, outside women's organizations, my family responsibilities, etc. My quiet times during this time were not what they should be, but now I find myself having regular, quality quiet time but feeling a lack of fulfillment. I don't seem to have any vision, and the Lord seems to be silent. Do you have any suggestions or scriptures?

A. The answer to your burnout problem and present lack of fulfillment is found in John 15:1,2: "*I am the true vine, and my Father is the husbandman. Every branch in me that beareth not fruit he taketh away: and every branch that beareth fruit, he purgeth it, that it may bring forth more fruit.*"

In every life there are seasons of bearing fruit, pruning, growing, and bearing more fruit. Certainly in the times of "fruit bearing," where there is evidence of what our life is producing, we have a sense of fulfillment because we can "see" what we have done.

However, there are necessary times when God puts us in a "dormant" state so that we can abide in Him and He in us: "*. . . As the branch cannot bear fruit of itself, except it abide in the vine; no more can ye, except ye abide in me*" (John 15:4). I believe you may be experiencing an "abiding time" in your life. God is giving you a season of rest, consolidation, and a chance to re-energize. Enjoy it! Receive this time as God's wisdom for this season in your life.

If the Lord is silent, then you can be certain that you are in His will! The Holy Spirit gets ''noisy'' within us when we begin to walk outside of God's will.

Q. There is a man who loves to argue in the Sunday school class my husband and I teach. It doesn't matter what the subject is or how we approach it; he is very vocal in his criticism of our understanding of the Bible and our presentation. No one else complains. The pastor has talked with him, but he continues to cause problems. What should we do?

A. You and your husband are being harassed by the devil, and you are being much too nice to him! Satan knows your potential and your heart for God, and he is doing everything he can to stop you. Take your God-given authority and power over Satan in Jesus' name, and command him to stop in his activity against you and your class.

After seeking God's guidance and wisdom, you need to go to this man and confront him in love but in firmness. You also need to forgive him and put the matter under the blood of Jesus; BUT this kind of disturbance needs to be stopped. This man is in rebellion by not coming under the leader's authority, whether it be you as a teacher, or the pastor. Satan will use him to bring dissension in the Body.

Brief comments and discussion that both build and enforce the teaching should always be welcome, IF time and circumstance permit; but negative and derogatory remarks are absolutely out of order. Follow the Biblical pattern in Matthew 18:15-20 in a spirit of meekness, and trust the Lord to resolve this problem.

You also have ministering spirits—angels—who are sent to perform the Word of God as you speak it from your lips. They will aid you in carrying out your authority based on God's Word.

Q. I know that God has a calling on my life either to preach or to teach so I quit my job because I didn't want anything to hold me back. Some doors have been opened, but I really need more financial support. Would it be all right for me to work part-time at a secular job?

A. Yes, you can be called to the ministry and still work at a secular job. There are many faithful men and women in the ministry today who are holding down full- or part-time jobs in order to support themselves. And in the Bible we find that it was the apostle Paul's custom to provide for his needs by working with his own hands (see II Thessalonians 3:8).

Q. Marilyn, I just don't understand how someone can be truly close to God, like David in the Bible, and still sin so terribly.

A. Being close to God does not make one exempt from sin. Saul, David, and Solomon certainly had the hand of God upon them, but as humans they were still given to temptation and sin. Like each of us, these great men had a choice—each day brought new opportunities either to be defeated or to be victorious. These Old Testament men did not have the New Testament covenant rights that we now have, which include understanding our authority and power through God's Word.

Because all humans have a sin nature, there is no person on earth who is exempt from temptation and sin. We have seen that in the Body of Christ when great men and women of God have been tempted and, in a time of weakness, have fallen. You have experienced this type of temptation and succumbed to sin, and so have I. Being in a leadership position often makes a person even more vulnerable because Satan has assigned demon spirits to tempt leaders and try to cause them to fall. That is why it is important for all of us to stay close to God through His Word, prayer, and fellowship with one another.

And always remember the good news that "*. . . The things which are impossible with men are possible with God*" (Luke 18:27). The word *possible* refers to "miracle-working power." The miracle-working power of God's grace can keep you in His righteousness.

Chapter Six
FRIENDSHIP

Q. I have a friend who is growing farther away from the Lord; our relationship has become strained. What can I do?

A. The very best advice I can give you on how to help your friend is to be a gap stander. I encourage you to spend some time praying in the Spirit for her. Perhaps you can even fast and pray for this relationship with the Lord to be restored. Fasting and prayer have broken many yokes in other peoples' lives. You'll also find your own faith strengthened to believe for her return to the Lord. So the most effective action you can take is to pray, pray, pray!

Q. My husband works with an alcoholic who is living with a man who is not her husband. She has repeatedly invited us to their home for dinner. Should we accept?

A. Jesus associated with men and women with poor reputations, and He told us to go into all the world to preach the gospel: *"The Son of man came eating and drinking, and they say, Behold a man gluttonous, and a winebibber, a friend of publicans and sinners. But wisdom is justified of her children"* (Matthew 11:19).

I believe the Lord wants you to carry your witness into this woman's home, even though she is an alcoholic and living with a man—certainly they both need the Lord, and you can bring Him to them! Do not be concerned by what other people may think of you—Jesus wasn't—but rather be concerned about the salvation of these two precious souls.

On the other hand, you should be certain that those people with whom you spend most of your time are fellow Christians. The Bible is very clear about the dangers of being unequally yoked with unbelievers, and that injunction definitely applies to all levels of relationships—business, marriage, and friendship (see II Corinthians 6:14).

Spiritual fellowship is a gift of God for those within the Body of Christ (Psalms 55:14; Galatians 2:9). Even the backslider is one who is out of fellowship with God; and therefore, our position should be to pray and believe that such a person will turn back to God. Let the Holy Spirit guide you in how much time to spend with unbelievers and what activities to share with them.

Q. I am so grieved about some friends of mine who have become involved in a false doctrine. Now they are harassing me with "intellectual" reasons why I should not believe the Bible as God's Word. What can I do?

A. The very first thing I want to tell you is, "Don't give up on your friends!" If you cannot speak to them about the subject and they will not take any literature, then pray this scripture for them: *"They also that erred in spirit shall come to understanding, and they that murmured shall learn doctrine"* (Isaiah 29:24).

Your friends have erred in their spirit, but you can pray this promise for them to return to right understanding. God says that those who have erred in spirit will learn the Word of God as a reality, and you can claim that scripture. My husband and I have stood on this scripture for friends and members of our church. It has sometimes taken months and even years, but over and over again we have seen God restore individuals to correct doctrine.

Don't argue with your friends, and don't listen to their false doctrines; but do keep praying the authority of God's Word over their lives. Then watch God enlighten the eyes of their understanding!

Q. Should we have pets, or do they take the time and place of people who need our attention?

A. Pets are a source of joy and comfort to many people. So long as their care and presence in our lives do not interfere with our relationship to God or hinder us in doing His will, I see nothing wrong with enjoying and caring for pets. The guideline we should follow in this regard is to ask ourselves if God and His kingdom have first place in our lives (Matthew 6:33).

Q. Marilyn, I'm confused by something Paul wrote in I Timothy 1:20. In referring to Hymenaeus and Alexander, were Paul's words, "I have delivered unto Satan," just a saying of his times or should we take this literally?

A. Paul also used this phrase in his letter to the Corinthians. A man was openly committing fornication and refused to repent. When Paul said to deliver him to Satan for the destruction of his flesh, he was telling the Church to withdraw their spiritual covering from this man. In other words, they were to stop fellowshiping with him and to let him reap the results of his sin. (See I Corinthians 5:1-11.)

Any member of the Church has God's supernatural covering as a result of the corporate anointing on the Body. When this covering is withdrawn, Satan can attack a person fully. I believe the action of disfellowshiping an individual should only be done through the authority of the church leadership—and then only under the very specific, strong direction of the Holy Spirit.

The good news is the end of the Corinthian story. We are told in II Corinthians 2:6-11 that this brother repented and was restored to fellowship with the Body of Christ.

Paul indicated in his letter to Timothy that Hymenaeus and Alexander were guilty of blasphemy. There is no record that they were ever restored to fellowship.

Q. Is it really Biblical to be "legally" married? I have a friend who loves the man she is living with very much, but they don't believe a marriage certificate is necessary because they are married to one another in their hearts.

A. The Bible is very clear that we are to obey the ordinances of our government: *"Submit yourselves to every ordinance of man for the Lord's sake: . . . For so is the will of God, that with well doing ye may put to silence the ignorance of foolish men: . . . "* (I Peter 2:13,15).

A marriage certificate is required by God because it is required by most states for a marriage to be legally binding. Without a marriage certificate, the rights of the individuals involved, and any children they may have, could be unprotected. God set up governments for the sake of order and law, and we are required to submit to those laws.

In the marriage ceremony vows of commitment are made to God and to the marriage partner. These vows are important, and the wedding ceremony is important. Jesus performed His first miracle at a wedding. Certainly, He believed that weddings were important.

Q. I am born again, but I still have friends who are not. Some of these people are in severe sexual bondages. How should I pray for them?

A. Christians overcome the enemy in two ways: first by the blood of the Lamb and next by the word of their testimony. The blood gives us authority to speak the Word over sin in our own life and in the lives of others. Confess the Word over those who are bound by sin. Pray that your friends will hunger and thirst after righteousness (Matthew 5:6), and then pray that they will confess their sins and receive God's forgiveness (I John 1:9). Thank God for His forgiveness and for the cleansing power of the blood.

Continue to stand in the gap for your friends, believing that nothing is too hard for God and His power can change things. Remember, Jesus came so that sin may no longer have dominion over us. God loves those who are bound by sin; and through the power of prayer, these people can know the liberty of walking in the light of the gospel.

Chapter Seven
MONEY

Q. My mother is 77 and has been told that receiving social security is wrong and that she should live with her children instead. She is quite capable and healthy. If she were otherwise, I would meet the need. Can you help my understanding?

A. There is no Biblical reason for your mother not to accept social security funds. It is a federally subsidized program that she or a loved one contributed to, and she is entitled to those benefits. It is very understandable that as she grows older, your mother may have a greater need to want her loved ones near; but that is no reason to deny herself this source of income.

Assuring her of your love and availability, should the need arise, will go a long way in alleviating any concerns she may have. I will pray with you that your mother will trust God as her ultimate security and rest in His Word that promises: *"But my God shall supply all your need according to his riches in glory by Christ Jesus"* (Philippians 4:19).

Q. I know we are to give to the poor, but how far do we go with this? There is a very poor family in our church; and it seems as though no matter how much my husband and I help them, they always need more. Neither of the adults work, and they don't seem to take very good care of the things that are given to them.

A. The apostle Paul had good words of advice about helping people financially: *"For even when we were with you, this we commanded you, that if any would not work, neither should he eat"* (II Thessalonians 3:10).

I believe we are wrong to give people money if they have not shown any accountability. Proverbs, the Old Testament book of wisdom, indicates that a sluggard—or a person not willing to work—will be motivated to work when they get hungry enough. So you will actually be motivating them to work by refusing to give them any more handouts. In the long run, this will be the most beneficial solution for both you and them. We should only give when directed by the Lord, and then our giving will ALWAYS be blessed.

If people request money from you and you believe the need is both genuine and directed of the Lord, ask them to give you a list. Then you buy those items as you are led by God. People who depend on handouts are often unable to make wise choices in purchasing and have little regard for the value of the gift since they did not earn it. Also the Bible tells us to do good especially to the household of faith (Galatians 6:10); so determine if your priorities on giving are in order before you offer any more assistance.

I know the Lord will bless you as you continue sowing with *wisdom* into His kingdom.

Q. My husband and I are in the process of taking out a mortgage on our home for some needed home improvements. I mentioned this to a sister who informed me that it is a sin to be in debt. Do you agree with her?

A. Many people believe that we should not borrow because of Romans 13:8: *"Owe no man any thing, but to love one another: for he that loveth another hath fulfilled the law."*

The phrase "owe no man any thing" is speaking of any type of debt that we can owe a person: financial, spiritual, moral, or otherwise. Financial debts are easily understood, but a spiritual debt is another matter. One way that we can have a "debt" with another person is by not forgiving them, or by violating their rights so that there is unforgiveness toward us. In that sense we "owe" them because we have violated their personal rights as an individual. Jesus says that we are to love one another (Matthew 22:39); and in loving one another, we will walk in forgiveness and do good in every aspect of our relationships. This is really what this scripture means.

There's nothing wrong with taking a mortgage out on a home

as long as one has the financial ability to repay the debt—payments must be made on time. If we were not supposed to borrow, then God would not have made provisions for borrowing in the Old Testament (Exodus 22:25). If it is a sin to borrow, then it would be a sin for God's people to lend; and there are many scriptures which give us specific instructions for lending (Leviticus 25:37; Deuteronomy 15:6,8; 23:19,20; Matthew 5:42; and Luke 6:34).

Q. I recently co-signed a loan for a good friend who desperately needed a car. Now I am told co-signing is not scriptural. Marilyn, why wouldn't it be scriptural to help a friend?

A. Proverbs 6:1,2; 11:15; 17:18; and 22:26 all warn against becoming ''surety'' for another person, because this will be a snare to us. The word *surety* means ''bondsman—one who co-signs or makes sure'' the debt will be paid. Your friend's debt could become your burden.

No matter how severe other people's financial needs are, do not react in pity and pick up the loose ends for them. You could be hindering God's work in their lives, and you could cause them to look to people, and not to God, for their answers.

Your friend needs to know that his/her ''surety'' is in God—not you.

Q. We co-signed with our daughter, a college student who has no credit, for a car. Is this different than co-signing for a friend?

A. I do not believe you were wrong in co-signing for your daughter. I don't believe the scriptures regarding co-signing refer to family members so long as a parent is willing and able to assume the payments in the event that the child defaults on the loan.

Q. How do I overcome the constant urge to charge items on credit. I'm always in debt, and it's even caused problems in our marriage. Do you have any pointers that will help me?

A. The first and most important step in overcoming an inordinate urge to charge items on credit is to (are you ready for this?) **cut up** your credit cards! This is the best way to remove temptation from this sin: *''But put ye on the Lord Jesus Christ, and make not provision for the flesh, to fulfil the lusts thereof''* (Romans 13:14). Your credit cards have been a ''provision for the flesh'' (in the sense that you lust to have material possessions). Make no provision for this uncontrollable desire.

Next, you must change your habits and thought patterns. Begin to study Proverbs and find scriptures which deal with debt and its consequences. Memorize these and meditate on them until they become a part of you. Finally, substitute your shopping habits for another activity, such as aerobic exercises or Bible studies with a friend.

When you *need* to shop, make a list. Once you have made your list, go over it once again and cross out all the items that are unnecessary. You might even want to have a second check by your husband to have him determine if the items on your list are really needs or just wants. Then when you shop, take along your husband or a friend who can help you remain accountable. When you shop, purchase only those items which are on your list, and **no** others! Discipline yourself to strictly follow your shopping lists, and your spending will never get out of hand again.

Another thing you must consider as you make your list is your budget. On the top of your list, put down exactly what you can spend according to the budget you and your husband set. If you stick with your budget, and your budget includes a debt-reduction program, eventually you will find yourself debt free—as well as free from a very expensive habit!

Q. Marilyn, why do you and other TV ministries ask for donations to be charged to a credit card? Isn't using a charge card really spending money not yet in hand?

A. Some people prefer the convenience of using a charge card because it saves them the time and expense of using checks. I see nothing wrong in the use of a charge card, *if it is not abused.*

Of course it is foolish to charge things when there are no finances to back it up. This will only create financial bondage. As in anything we do, we must use wisdom (Colossians 1:9).

Q. Should I save for retirement, or would that be storing up treasures on earth?

A. The Bible does not teach that saving is wrong: "*The ants are a people not strong, yet they prepare their meat in the summer*" (Proverbs 30:25). A retirement fund or a savings account would be wise management of the funds that God has given you. God is never offended when we are good stewards of those gifts which He has entrusted to our keeping.

Q. My husband and I own a small cafe that is open 7 days a week from 6 a.m. to 10 p.m. We are rarely able to go to church; our three children see very little of us; we make just enough to keep up the business and household expenses and our tithing. I really want to spend more time with our children, but I'm not sure the cafe will make it without me there. What should I do?

A. Because I love you, I am going to speak very frankly. I sense that you are torn between your feelings of loyalty toward your husband and your responsibilities toward your children. However, there is a difference between ministering to your husband's needs and helping him with his work. God must be first in your life, your husband's personal needs second, and your children third. Your church should be your fourth priority followed by your job, or in your case, your husband's job.

Scripturally, you must take care of your children and meet their needs. Your children's future depends on this, or they may develop bitter attitudes and a sense that they are unloved by you and your husband. If the restaurant comes before them, they will sense this and their own values could become distorted.

I suggest you read Proverbs 31, and let that become a standard for your life. Let the Holy Spirit minister to you and show you how you can actually save money. There is nothing wrong with working outside the home if your children are receiving godly care. However, if the Holy Spirit is leading you to stay home, you must be obedient. Ask God to speak to your husband and show him how important this is and that in a few years, as your children grow older, they can easily become a part of the business and help you with the restaurant. It can become a ''family'' business!

The second advantage I see to you giving your children the care that they need is that I believe your finances will fall in line. If your household is in order, God can then put your finances in order. Anytime we have a financial problem, it is important for us to stop and seek God as to why we are not being financially blessed. Usually it is because something is out of line in our own lives; and in your case, it seems to be that your children need you right now.

When we are tithing, God promises in Malachi 3 that He will rebuke the devourer on our behalf, and that He will ''open heaven'' with financial blessings. Begin confessing this scripture for your family and business—and watch God work!

Q. Is it all right for Christians to have insurance or does it show a lack of faith in God?

A. In this present world of evil, sin, and sickness, I believe that God calls for us to use wisdom in every area of our life. Insurance is one of these areas. Because the Bible is silent on this subject, each person has been left to decide for himself whether it is right or wrong. Personally, I believe it is good wisdom to have insurance. God wants us to make sure that our families are well cared for, and we are being good stewards of our finances. So the decision is yours. Pray and ask the Holy Spirit to lead you in your individual situation.

Q. I recently received a permanent and a haircut and both were done very poorly. They said I could have the permanent redone; however, my hair was not in good enough condition. So I asked for my money back. Was this the right thing to do?

A. As Christians we need to be wise as serpents and harmless as doves (Matthew 10:16). Anytime we enter into a business agreement such as you described and the agreement is not met or the services are not performed up to expectations, we have a right to have that situation corrected, or to receive a full refund when the services are poorly performed. Sometimes Christians don't take their full authority over worldly financial principles and let themselves be taken advantage of.

Before work is begun, it is wise to be sure that you and the person you are doing business with know exactly what work is to be done, what it will cost, and what you can do if things are not satisfactory. Whenever possible, a written agreement is good. When we pay for a service, we should get what we pay for. If we do not get it, we should not pay for it.

Q. Is it all right for Christians to gamble? Our state lottery funds help provide many services.

A. I definitely believe that it is wrong for Christians to gamble: *"Wealth gotten by vanity shall be diminished: but he that gathereth by labour shall increase"* (Proverbs 13:11). Christians are to trust God to supply their needs, not the state lottery or any other form of gambling (Jeremiah 17:11; Philippians 4:19).

In every game of chance, there is only one winner but many losers. Gambling has cost many families the very food that they should have had to put in their mouths. It has also caused great grief and heartache: *"A man shall not be established by wickedness:* . . . " (Proverbs 12:3). Often people have begun gambling because they did not want to work. The Bible clearly tells us that we should be satisfied with the labor of our own hands (Proverbs 12:11).

I would not encourage Christians to buy lottery tickets, but I certainly don't think it is an unforgivable sin. Let every man do in his own heart that which does not condemn him. You might want to meditate upon the scriptures I've given you to help you in this matter.

Q. What is tithing and is it the same as an offering?

A. The Hebrew word for *tithe* literally means "tenth or ten percent." We "owe" God the first ten percent of our income which is called the tithe.

Offerings are what we give above and beyond the tithe. The tithe is only the beginning! Your offerings are your financial seeds planted into the kingdom of God. There are various categories of offerings such as: first fruit offerings, almsgiving, and sacrificial giving. I believe that Jesus was talking of offerings when He said: *"Give, and it shall be given unto you; good measure, pressed down, and shaken together, and running over, shall men give unto your bosom* . . . " (Luke 6:38).

Q. Why should Christians have to tithe since tithing is an Old Testament law?

A. The book of Hebrews is very definitely new covenant scripture, and Hebrews 7:2 tells us Abraham paid tithes to Melchizedek long before the law was given. Tithing is a principle taught throughout the Scriptures, before and after the Mosaic law. Since it is a principle of God, it was included in the law. Acts 20:35 says it is more blessed to give than to receive. The word *blessed* here means "to cause to prosper." Our tithe opens the door to God's blessing.

Matthew 23:23 indicates that Jesus assumed tithes should be paid: "*. . . ye pay tithe of mint and anise and cummin, and have omitted the weightier matters of the law, judgment, mercy, and faith: these ought ye to have done, and not to leave the other undone.*" The "other" He was referring to was the matter of tithes.

Q. I really want to pay our tithes, but my husband says we can't afford to give that much to the church. I'm afraid we're missing God's blessings for us; so is it all right if I tithe and just not tell my husband?

A. Two wrongs don't make a right, so don't go behind your husband's back to tithe or give offerings. I advise you to talk to your husband again; but before you do, be sure you have spent lots of time praying about this situation. Take the time to make an itemized list of all of your expenses, as well as his. Ask the Lord to show you a budget for your total income where you can tithe, put something into savings, and pay your other expenses. Perhaps when your husband sees these figures on paper, he will realize how God has blessed you with the handling of the household finances. Be sure to approach your husband in a positive way—build him up by telling him all the ways you appreciate him, and he will be ready to listen.

Chapter Eight
HEALTH AND HEALING

Q. Does God still heal people today? I've heard that physical healing was just for the first-century Church.

A. Yes, God still heals people today! I've heard that rumor about the first-century Church, too; but I can tell you that God loves us just as much as He loved those Christians. Jesus' final words to His disciples included this promise: *"And these signs shall follow them that believe; In my name shall they cast out devils; . . . they shall lay hands on the sick, and they shall recover"* (Mark 16:17,18).

I've seen many, many healings take place, and I've experienced healing in my own body as well. It often takes consistency in prayer, standing on the Word, and persistent patience.

Sometimes people plant the healing "seeds" of God's Word at an advanced stage of illness, and the death process is too far advanced for the life of God's Word to manifest. It is important to plant God's Word in our hearts before Satan ever tries to attack us with sickness so that the roots of sickness and disease will have no place in our lives. This is one reason people are sometimes not healed. There are many other reasons, and we don't know each individual's discouragement or level of faith for healing. The important thing is to remember that God's Word is ALWAYS true, and the Word is our standard of truth.

The Scriptures are loaded with dynamite promises for healing. Among these promises are Exodus 15:26; Psalms 91; 103:3; Proverbs 4:20-23; Isaiah 53:4,5; Malachi 4:2; Matthew 8:16,17; Galatians 3:13; I Peter 2:24; and III John 2.

Q. Marilyn, do you believe that the presence of sickness in the body indicates that the person is not a Christian?

A. I do not believe that the presence of sickness in the body indicates that the person is not a Christian. But God has two wonderful truths from His Word that should be a comfort and a hope to us: (1) physical healing is part of the redemptive work of our Lord Jesus Christ (see I Peter 2:24), and (2) there is no condemnation for any Christian who has not entered into the fullness of what God has provided (see Romans 8:1).

Q. When hands are being laid on me for healing, what should I think about?

A. When you are in a healing line, it is important to keep your thoughts on Jesus and His healing promises—not the minister. People will fail you, but Jesus never fails. If you look to man, you will be disappointed; if you trust in God's Word, it will not fail.

Q. Can Satan heal people?

A. Since all sickness, disease, and infirmity are from Satan (Luke 13:16; Acts 10:38), he has no difficulty in removing it; but he has no *creative* power to heal. However, the devil is also the world's most accomplished liar. In his efforts to enslave people in his kingdom, Satan will use any available tool, including a counterfeit healing.

Q. Marilyn, I heard you talking about daily health scriptures. What did you mean?

A. I'm sure you know that Jesus was anointed with power to heal those oppressed of the devil (Acts 10:38); you may even be sure that healing is of God. Well, now I want to help you see that walking in *divine health* is even better! That's why I take my daily dose of health scriptures—I speak scriptures that affirm the divine health that God wants for my life. Some scriptures that you can use for this purpose are Psalms 91:10; Proverbs 3:8; 4:20,22; 16:24; and Romans 6:13.

As you confess scriptures like these, they are like a prescription of healing from the Lord. I know that these scriptures will not go forth in your life and return void; I am absolutely certain that they will produce health for you.

Q. I have prayed and prayed for healing, but I still have the symptoms of my disease. Why haven't I been healed?

A. Sometimes when believers lay hands on sick people, the healing manifests instantly. It is a wonderful miracle; but when someone doesn't recover immediately, it is important to keep your faith in God's Word and not look at the symptoms.

When healing takes a period of time, it is important to understand that God's Word works like a seed planted in your spirit. When you plant a carrot seed, you don't run outside the next day expecting to pull carrots! It is sometimes necessary to stand in faith for a long time; but as you continue to stand, the day will come when healing is evident because the seed will have matured.

We know that all sickness and disease originated with the devil (Acts 10:38), and sometimes demonic personalities manifest various diseases or disorders in people. Nevertheless, believers have power and authority given by Christ to rebuke any such thing (Luke 10:18,19). When you are praying for yourself or another, ''cover all the bases'' by coming against Satan and any demonic activity that may be present as well as speaking the healing Word of God to the body and soul. I know an evangelist who comes against all sickness, disease, and infirmity as though it comes directly from evil spirits; and he has unusual success. You do have the victory over all these things in the name of Jesus (I John 3:8).

Q. Is it an indication of unbelief for me to follow the instruction of a physician and not lean solely on God?

A. First of all, God is your healer (Psalms 103:2,3); and you should depend upon Him, through the promises of His Word, to perform healing on your behalf.

However, that does not mean that you are wrong to take advantage of a doctor's knowledge. Jesus said that the sick have need of a physician (Matthew 9:12; Mark 2:17; and Luke 5:31). We need to use balance and wisdom in every area of our life, and I believe it is only good wisdom to use modern medicine to aid in the healing of our bodies.

I want to reiterate that all healing comes from God. Sometimes healing comes in a supernatural manner; sometimes it comes through the natural processes of healing with the assistance of the medical profession. Either way, the healing is from Him and He is to receive the glory for it.

Q. I know a man who had a kidney transplant and then stopped taking the medication which prevents rejection of the transplanted kidney. He did this because he is believing for healing; but over the past few months, his blood tests have shown that his kidney function is decreasing. I feel that the Lord gave this man his healing through the successful acceptance of this organ into his body. Should he have stopped taking his medication?

A. I always encourage people to continue to follow their doctor's orders until the healing has completely manifested. Unless God has given very clear direction to do otherwise, I believe it is foolish presumption to disregard sound medical instruction. We do not negate our faith by continuing to take medicine *with* God's Word.

Q. For almost ten years I have had a sleeping problem. I've examined my heart, and it seems to be at peace with God. I don't want to take sleeping pills, but I do occasionally. Please help me if you can.

A. I would encourage prayer instead of sleeping pills, since the results will be longer lasting: *"It is vain for you to rise up early, to sit up late, to eat the bread of sorrows: for so he giveth his beloved sleep"* (Psalms 127:2). You can claim this scripture if you feel that it is simply the cares of this world which are pressing in on you and robbing you of sleep. Be sure to cast all your cares upon Him because He cares for you. God loves you and wants you to have the proper rest; so stand on the Word, and He will give you rest.

If the insomnia (the inability to sleep) continues, then I recommend you pray and intercede at night. If you commit yourself to prayer whenever you're awakened, then the devil won't continue to harass you if he is the cause of your sleeplessness. If it is the Father, then more than likely your wakefulness is a call to prayer, and you need to respond quickly when you find yourself awake. Either way, you win!

Q. I know of healing ministries that use deliverance from anxiety, guilt, etc., which then releases deliverance for physical ailments. What do you think of this, Marilyn?

A. There is a definite place for the deliverance ministry according to Mark 16:17. We are told to cast out devils in the name of Jesus, but we must be careful not to get out of balance in this area. We need to be both very sensitive and led of the Lord in the area of deliverance. Of course, Satan is behind all evil, but deliverance is not always the answer for every sickness. There are other types of prayer which will release healing for individuals, such as the prayer found in James 5:13,14 or the laying on of hands found in Mark 16:18. There are many ways to minister healing, and one has to be led of the Spirit in order to know which to use.

Q. When a Christian has been healed of a supposedly incurable disease, how should he or she answer the sort of questions asked by insurance companies and health organizations? I expect to change jobs soon, so the subject of my medical history will arise. I want to be truthful; so shall I just trust God that I won't be asked? Or is there an answer I can give?

A. I would suggest that you go to a doctor who doesn't know you or your medical history, and get a complete examination and diagnosis from him. If he indeed declares you free from this disease, you can use his report and give a truthful history. However, if a second medical opinion confirms the first, I would encourage you to be truthful in your interview by simply telling them that you believe God has healed you of this disease and the symptoms are leaving. Perhaps you can even get a medical report of your improvement. In any case, be honest with your past history and be bold about your testimony as well! This may open an excellent door for you to witness to these people.

Q. Is it wrong to place one's parents in a nursing home?

A. This is such a sensitive issue that it must be prayerfully considered and discussed with the person involved—if they are mentally capable of helping in such a decision. It is so important to follow the leading of the Holy Spirit so neither rejection nor condemnation will have an opportunity to take root.

No one doubts the importance of honoring one's parents. The problem is what is the best way to do that? When a person comes to a point where they are no longer able to care for their elderly parents because of the parents' physical needs, then there is nothing wrong with placing them where they can receive appropriate care. However, no one should be put away because the family just doesn't want to bothered with them anymore. No matter what age your parents may be, they should be treated in the same way that you will want to be treated when you are their age.

Q. What should a Christian's position be on the use of life support systems?

A. The Scriptures do not deal directly with "life support systems"; however, I believe we can gain great understanding about this issue by looking at the Biblical view of death. Satan is the one who kills; and Jesus gives abundant life: *"The thief cometh not, but for to steal, and to kill, and to destroy: I am come that they might have life, and that they might have it more abundantly"* (John 10:10). The Bible also declares that death is an enemy of God (I Corinthians 15:26).

I believe it always has been and always will be God's will for a person to live a long, prosperous life. You will also find within the physician's code of ethics the determination to maintain and sustain life as long as possible. Straying from this view gets one into the concept of *euthanasia*, which means "mercy killing." When *men* start deciding who should live or who should die, I believe they get into an area that should be reserved for God. And we know that He has chosen life!

If a person is unsaved, then I believe we should do everything possible to keep that soul from going to hell—sustain the physical life on life support systems—and pray for a miracle, so that the person can receive Jesus. However, when a doctor has determined that a person is absolutely clinically dead, then that is a different matter. A Christian who is clinically dead need no longer be held on life support systems, *unless the Holy Spirit absolutely directs otherwise.*

Q. Is it okay to donate organs? Is there anything in the Bible that says I should not leave my body to science?

A. I see nothing wrong with donating organs to science. First Corinthians 15:35-55 states that though our bodies are sown as corruptible, they will be raised as incorruptible. Our new bodies will not be the same as our present bodies which are under the law of sin and death. If you think logically, these present bodies will decay and disintegrate. In any case, this is a personal decision each person must make for himself through the guidance of the Holy Spirit.

Q. Can a person die and come back to life? Can you give me Scripture to support your point of view?

A. I believe that people can have a death experience and return to life to tell about it. Acts 14:19,20 gives us the example of Paul's death by stoning and his being raised from the dead through the prayers of some disciples. In addition, both Elisha and Elijah—not to mention, Jesus—raised people from the dead.

Q. What does eating and drinking damnation in I Corinthians 11 mean?

A. Paul made a very strong statement in I Corinthians 11:27-30 that because people fail to acknowledge the power that Jesus imparted through His resurrection, some are weak and sick and some have even died. Why? Because they ate and drank damnation to themselves by not receiving what God had offered through the Lord's Supper. It is so important for Christians to stop seeing Communion as merely a one-day ritual. They must receive it as God's eternal power to heal and strengthen them as well as lengthen their life spans.

Another common reason that Christians fail to receive this resurrection power is because they are ''picking'' at each other. Instead of picking, we should allow the bread of resurrection to unite us in Christ. We will stop picking at each other when we are feasting on the bread of God's resurrection power—instead of complaining about one another. We don't feel happy when guests at our dinner table pick at the food, and neither should we pick at one another when we are at the Lord's table. We are all one body in Christ Jesus.

Q. I don't understand what Paul meant when he talked about his thorn in the flesh. Was this some kind of sickness that was part of God's will for Paul's life?

A. Through a study of the Scriptures, I have found thorns to be those persons who buffeted God's people (see Numbers 33:55 and Judges 2:3). Personally, I believe the Jews who harassed and persecuted Paul for the sake of the gospel of Christ were a "real pain in the neck"—his thorn in the flesh. Second Corinthians 12:7 tells us that Paul's thorn in the flesh was a messenger of Satan which was sent to buffet him. Because this was a messenger of Satan, we very clearly know that this thorn was not from God. Therefore, it was NOT God's will for Paul. No messenger of Satan can ever be part of God's will or plan.

God's will was that His strength would be made perfect in Paul and that the power of Christ would rest upon Paul. Obviously, Paul understood this: "*. . . for when I am weak, then am I strong*" (II Corinthians 12:10). Paul knew that it is in God's power that we come against these messengers of Satan in our lives—not through our own power and might, but by the might of the Holy Spirit.

When God told Paul that His "grace was sufficient," He was saying that the authority and power (grace) that had been given to Paul was sufficient power to command the messenger of Satan to leave. God's grace is sufficient to handle anything Satan sends against us!

Chapter Nine

HABITS AND DELIVERANCE

Q. What is a yoke of bondage? Is this what Jesus said we should take in Matthew 11:29?

A. A yoke is what joins two oxen together to make them more easily directed by a farmer. Jesus said we should take His yoke so we could be joined to other believers, and then Jesus can lead us in one direction.

The Bible does speak of another type of yoke, but it is one Christ wants to free us from—a yoke of bondage (Galatians 5:1). The word ''yoke'' has three meanings: to join yourself with something in order to work; to couple two things together; and a pair of balances.

If you are yoked to Jesus Christ, your Christian walk will be marked by temperance or balance. But the yoke of sin is one of ups and downs, which will keep you out of balance. Your goal in the freedom of the Spirit-filled life ought to be one where all your attitudes and actions are consistent with God's Word. Any other yoke will distract from your call, become a bondage, and a hard task master.

Q. Marilyn, why do you teach that Christians shouldn't drink alcohol? God asked for a tithe of the wine in Deuteronomy 14:23, and Paul told Timothy to take wine for his stomach.

A. The Scriptures do indicate that the Old Testament people of God were allowed to drink *temperately.* They were also allowed to end their marriages through divorce; however, Jesus said that was because of the hardness of their hearts, not because it was God's best for them (see Matthew 19:8,9). There are many other scriptures which warn believers against the use of alcoholic beverages (Proverbs 20:1; 23:29-35; Isaiah 5:11; 28:7; Habakkuk 2:15; Luke 21:34.)

In addition there were at least two special groups that were absolutely advised not to drink wine or other "strong drink": priests (Leviticus 10:9,10) and kings (Proverbs 31:4,5). Jesus said He has made believers as kings and priests to God (Revelation 1:6); and therefore, it is scriptural for Christians to abstain from the use of alcohol.

There are several Greek words that have been translated as "wine," including unfermented grape juice. Such a "wine" may be purchased in Israel today. Some Biblical scholars have suggested that it would be better to use the English phrase "juice of the vine" instead of "wine." Paul was advising Timothy not to drink water any longer but to use a little wine for his stomach's sake. Timothy was evidently troubled by stomach problems which was not unusual in a society which did not have the ability to purify their water the way we do. Wine, both fermented and unfermented, was recognized as an appropriate remedy for some digestive problems. In our modern era, most people have access to pure water and more effective medications.

In a day when alcoholism is such a problem, we should make sure our behavior does not cause a brother to stumble. A Christian need only look at the results of alcohol consumption in our society to make a wise and proper decision not to drink. (See Romans 14:17-21.)

Q. Is there such a thing as a spirit of alcoholism?

A. Yes, there is a spirit of alcoholism, which will enter anyone's life if given the opportunity. However, Jesus is seated in heavenly places *far above* all demonic rulers and authorities, and they are under His feet (Ephesians 1:19-23). And what's even more wonderful is that *we* are seated *with Him* in those heavenly places, and demons and occult powers are under our feet as well (Ephesians 2:4-6)!

Q. Will cigarettes be allowed in heaven? I love God and I'm sure He loves me. However, I have been smoking since I was 11, and I don't want to quit.

A. I am glad that you love the Lord and understand that He loves you. Nevertheless, I must tell you that there will be no smoking in heaven. The Bible tells us that our bodies are the temples of God (I Corinthians 6:19), and we are to "... *cleanse ourselves from all filthiness of the flesh and spirit, perfecting holiness in the fear of God*" (II Corinthians 7:1).

Smoking is not a clean habit, and it has been proven to be so bad for your health that it often shortens the lives of those who smoke. This means that not only are smokers robbed of the blessings which God has for them in this life but others are robbed of the ministry those smokers could have brought. Smoking is also an expensive habit that takes finances which could be used to feed the poor, clothe the naked, and spread the gospel of Jesus Christ.

I suggest that you pray to be able to relinquish this habit to the Lord. Ask Him to reveal to you how He feels about it. Really make an effort to spend more time in the Word and in prayer, developing a relationship with the Lord; and then let the Lord deal with you openly. Only the conviction that comes from the Lord will ever convince you that you should quit.

Q. How can I break the habit of sleeping too long in the morning? I sleep soundly, sometimes not hearing alarms or even turning them off in my sleep!

A. Above all, do not get under condemnation about your inability to arise early in the morning. If you get under condemnation, you will cripple your spirit man, who is able to aid you in your desire to do this. Relax in the Lord, and continue to confess scriptures over yourself about waking early in the morning—scriptures such as Psalms 57:8 and Proverbs 8:17. Believe in your heart that the Lord will enable you to do this.

Most adults require seven to eight hours of sleep, but many people can get by with much less, depending on their metabolism and lifestyle. Proverbs 31 indicates that a diligent woman who rises early is one who rises while it is yet night (Proverbs 31:15 NAS). So it is wise to rise before sunrise to begin your day with the Lord. Although we should not get into bondage over a certain time, we do need to be sensitive to the leading of the Holy Spirit in this area and not be slothful in our waking habits.

Q. My mother and brother believe that it is unscriptural for a person who is overweight to minister to others because that person doesn't have control of his own life. Is this correct?

A. Paul outlined the qualifications for church leaders in I Timothy chapters 2 and 3. I see nothing wrong with ministering even when one is overweight. Each of us has weaknesses and sins in our lives, but we are still commanded to minister. If we waited until we were sinless, there would be no one ministering! I agree that it is important to lead a self-disciplined life; but at the same time, we must cover each other in love and not be critical.

Sometimes it's too easy to compare ourselves with other Christians. But II Corinthians 10:12 tells us that it isn't wise for Christians to do that. Looking at others encourages us to grade ourselves "on a curve," but God grades us by His Word. When you look at Christians—even overweight Christians—look for the image of Jesus inside and see their full potential in Him. Your faith for that potential can help bring it about in someone's life.

Q. My daughter has been diagnosed as anorexic. How can I use the Bible to help her get over this affliction?

A. The Bible definitely gives hope for people with eating disorders. These people suffer because they have set up false images of themselves in their minds. They have an image of themselves as fat, when in reality they are very thin. This is a false image, actually a false idol.

Your daughter's first step must be to receive Jesus as her Savior or to rededicate her life if she is already saved. Either step needs to include repentance for the sin of idolatry. If she is not ready to do this, then you need to pray that God will soften her heart and send others to witness to her. Often a stranger can reach our loved ones when they will not listen to us. Be sure to seek God's wisdom for how to handle every step of your daughter's deliverance.

After she has given her life to Jesus, your daughter will need to have you and other believers stand with her to bind and rebuke, in Jesus' name, any demonic influences and deceptions that have attempted to destroy her life through this eating disorder. Be sure to pray for total healing of her mind, emotions, and body. Help your daughter find scriptures that affirm the fact that she is loved and accepted by God. Such a list would probably include: Psalms 107:20; 139:14; Zephaniah 3:17; I Corinthians 2:14-16; Philippians 4:7; and I Thessalonians 3:13. As she meditates on these scriptures and prays these promises for herself, her mind will be renewed and healed.

I also want to encourage you to seek godly counseling for your daughter. The results of freedom may be seen quickly or they may take awhile; but be assured that deliverance is near! I have personally known many believers who have been completely set free from this type of eating disorder.

Q. How do you feel, Marilyn, about taking vitamins and eating health foods for healing? I've heard that this is a part of holistic medicine, and therefore New Age.

A. First of all, God is our healer; and I depend upon Him to perform healing on my behalf. However, I see nothing wrong with taking vitamins and eating a healthy diet because God created this natural means for both maintaining our health and healing our bodies.

Q. I just don't seem to be able to lose weight. Marilyn, does the Bible offer any help with this problem?

A. The Bible has a great deal to say about eating; but it is very important that you take your eyes off your weight problem and keep them on God. You must not let anyone, including yourself, put you down because you have not yet gained the victory in this area. Jesus promised that as we seek the kingdom, all things will be added to us. I believe that includes victory over your weight.

There are several very practical steps that will help you as you learn to rest in the Lord in this area: (1) Keep your mind active by thinking on right things (Philippians 4:8). (2) Don't eat to stuff yourself but to satisfy yourself (Proverbs 13:25). (3) Watch your intake of sweets and meats (Proverbs 23:3,20). (4) When you eat, do it to glorify God (I Corinthians 10:31). (5) Take your bad eating habits to the Cross and reckon them dead (Proverbs 23:2). (6) Pray in the Spirit for ten minutes before you sit down to eat (Romans 8:26,27). (7) Speak right words about your food before you eat (Proverbs 18:20). (8) Don't eat when you are depressed (Proverbs 15:15). (9) Pray God's Word over your food (Philippians 4:6; I Timothy 4:4,5).

Q. I have struggled with lying my entire life. Please tell me how to get deliverance from this.

A. In order to deal with a habit of lying, you must first bind the lying spirits that operate through you. Resist them in Jesus' name. Then find all the scriptures you can about truth, and meditate upon them "day and night." Here are some you can start with—Psalms 86:11; 89:14; 119:30; Proverbs 3:3; 8:7; John 8:32; 16:13. Memorize these scriptures so that you can think about them wherever you are. Plant them so deeply in your heart that they will bear fruit and begin to take dominion in your life.

Each time the Holy Spirit convicts you of lying, immediately repent and speak the truth—speak one of the scriptures that you have learned. Remember that if we confess our sins, God is faithful and just to forgive us and cleanse us from *all* unrighteousness (I John 1:9). Each time you confess that you have lied, God not only will give you grace to cleanse this sin from your life but also grace to speak the truth in love. This is a process which will take time, but be persistent, and you will win!

Q. How can I develop a prayer habit? I've tried, but I don't seem to be able to stick with it. Also, how much time should I be spending in prayer and studying the Word?

A. You will have to ask the Holy Spirit how much time you should spend in these areas. Depending on the level of spiritual growth and the need for fellowship with Him, you'll find the Lord requires different quantities of time for different individuals.

A good "measure" to go by is found in Mark 14:37,38. While Jesus was in the Garden of Gethsemane on the night of His betrayal, He asked the disciples to watch and pray with Him for one hour. This can be a call for us to pray and study at least one hour each day, depending upon the leading of the Holy Spirit.

In order to be faithful, one has to make a quality commitment. I can guarantee you that the rewards for making this kind of commitment are worth the price you will pay. There is an old saying that may help you understand the importance of self-discipline in this area: "Sow a thought, reap an action; sow an action, reap a habit; sow a habit, reap a destiny."

If it is a struggle to devote one hour of your time each day, then start with fifteen minutes—*the key is consistency, not length*. As you are faithful in short periods, you will find yourself wanting to spend more and more time with Jesus. As this relationship grows, it will become a joy and not a chore.

Q. So many bad things seem to "run" in my family. I believe these may be curses. Can I pray and break them for the entire family?

A. Family curses can be broken for your family, but not for individuals who are unwilling. However, God can change an unwilling heart as you intercede and ask God to soften that heart.

Though we are under grace, we suffer from sickness, disease, death, and even generational bondages! We have eternal salvation, but we aren't in heaven yet; so we must *appropriate* the freedom Christ gave us (Galatians 3:13). We have to drive off the "giants" of generational bondages just as the Hebrew children had to drive the giants out of the land that God gave to them.

The good news is we **can** be free from these curses through Jesus' redemptive blood. Simply command the curse to be broken in the name of Jesus and speak the blood of Jesus over your family, which will cleanse them from all unrighteousness. Some additional scriptures concerning this are Deuteronomy 27,28; Job 31:30; Psalms 68:6; Romans 8:28.

Q. I heard you say that your Dad had a nervous breakdown, but you seem so strong and healthy. My grandfather, my brother, and I have all had nervous breakdowns. What is your secret?

A. When I was younger, Satan told me, "Your grandfather had a breakdown; your father had a breakdown; and you're going to have a nervous breakdown."

I began to think, "Well, it runs in the family, so I'm probably going to have a breakdown." About this same time, the Lord reminded me that He is my Father and He's *never* had a nervous breakdown! He showed me that this was a generation curse; and because the blood of Jesus Christ has cleansed me from all unrighteousness, including all family curses, I am no longer under the curse.

God has assured me that not only will I never have a breakdown but my children will never have a breakdown because I have claimed the blood of Jesus and broken that curse in His name. Praise God, the curse is broken!

Q. At the end of II Peter 3:18, we're told to "grow in grace." How do you grow in grace?

A. The Bible has given us many ways in which we can grow in grace. For instance, the word *edify* means "to grow spiritually." One of the ways that we can grow in this kind of grace is by praying in the Holy Spirit (Romans 8:26; I Corinthians 14:2-15; Jude 20). Another way that we grow is through reading and meditating on the Word of God. (Romans 10:17; I Peter 2:2.) If you wish to get further insight on this type of growth, I would encourage you to do a word study on *growth* by using Strong's Concordance or another study tool. You can purchase such books at any Bible bookstore. I know your personal study will be well rewarded!

Chapter Ten

PRAYER AND FASTING

Q. I've noticed that corporate prayer (unity in prayer with others in the Body of Christ) strengthens us. Why is that?

A. Corporate prayer and unity with others in the Body of Christ is strengthening because of the corporate anointing that is upon the Body. When we join a church and become involved and committed in that particular Body, there is a special covering which God places upon it because it is a part of His established plan for the Church. Deuteronomy 32:30 promises that one person can put a thousand to flight, but two will put ten thousand demons to flight. The power of our prayers dramatically increases with the prayer of agreement.

People who hop from church to church open themselves to attacks from Satan, who is compared to a wolf in the Bible. In the natural, the only time a wolf attacks is when a sheep has strayed and is not protected by a flock. Wolves pick up sheep one by one, and they do this by trying to separate the sheep from the flock. As long as you are with the flock, there is protection because a wolf knows that where there is a flock, there is a shepherd; and Satan does not want to tackle the Good Shepherd—Jesus!

Q. I would like to have a better understanding of "standing in the gap." Do you believe that one can "stand in the gap" for more than one person?

A. Standing in the gap has to do with us sending God's strength and protection to fill in where the hedge (a protective wall) has been broken down or weakened by Satan. Since God indwells us, we have that protection that is spoken of in Job 1:10: *"Hast not thou made an hedge about him, and about his house, and about all that he hath on every side? thou hast blessed the work of His hands, and his substance is increased in the land."*

God has that kind of hedge available to us all, but we know

that too often the enemy blinds us and causes a "gap in the hedge." We can then, through prayer, bring the strength and power of God to make that hedge strong, by believing and confessing the Word over all the situations that are made known to us: *"And I sought for a man among them, that should make up the hedge, and stand in the gap before me for the land, that I should not destroy it: but I found none"* (Ezekiel 22:30).

God is looking for someone like you and me to "stand in the gap." Another way we "fill a gap" is the gap between an unsaved person and God. Through prayer, we can be the bridge that takes hold of God with one hand and the unsaved person with the other—bringing God's touch and salvation to the lost. So we can and should stand in the gap for many.

Q. Could you please explain to me why you think "speaking the Word" is so vital for Christians? Can speaking God's promises over a situation really change the situation or person?

A. The reason that speaking the Word is so vital to the Christian walk is because the Bible says that "*. . . the Word of God is living and active and sharper than any two-edged sword, . . .*" (Hebrews 4:12 NAS). By speaking the Word, we activate the power that is contained within it in the same way we activate a seed when we plant it into the ground. The spoken Word of God will produce power and life because that is the very nature of God. When we speak His Word, it is like planting seed in our hearts.

The Scriptures tell us that His Word is near us to transform situations when we believe it and speak it. Jesus takes to the Father the Word which we speak as a guarantee of His promises (Hebrews 3:1; 4:14; 10:23). When we pray the promises and believe as we pray that we have our answer, God moves on behalf of His Word (Mark 11:23,24).

Prayer is not a way to manipulate people or circumstances. When we speak God's promises to Him and to situations, we release God's power to accomplish blessing and change. God can rearrange circumstances, open hearts, and move mountains.

The Bible tells us in I John 5:14,15 that if God *hears* us, then He will *answer* us, and that He hears us when we pray according to His will. The way to pray according to His will is to find a promise in the Bible for your situation, and pray that promise to God. In this way your prayers will always be answered (see II Corinthians 1:20).

Q. What do ministers or others pray (or say) over their children before the children leave for school, etc.?

A. The best thing to pray over your children are scriptures which deal with a particular situation—whether it be for protection, for wisdom, or whatever the circumstances might be. Here are some scriptures to pray over your children and their future: Psalms 23; John 6:37; 10:27-29; Romans 8:38,39; Philippians 1:6; II Thessalonians 3:3; I Peter 2:3-5.

When I pray for my children, I will take a verse such as II Thessalonians 3:3 and pray it in this way: *"But the Lord is faithful who will establish (child's name) and keep (child's name) from evil."* I personalize the prayers for myself and my family in order to make these scriptures personal to the children as well as making them specific with the Lord. If we ask for nothing in particular, we get nothing in particular! Let me suggest that you do a Bible search and find scriptures that you would particularly like to see fulfilled in your own children's lives.

Q. Why do some people address the devil rather than God when they are praying?

A. Taking our authority and addressing Satan directly is a pattern which Jesus established during His earthly ministry. When Jesus took authority over demons, He spoke to them directly because authority had been given to Him. Jesus delegated this same authority to us, and He will not violate the authority which we have been given. It is unscriptural to ask the Father to take care of the devil for us—He told us to do it. I want to encourage you to get a book titled THE BELIEVER'S AUTHORITY, by Kenneth Hagin. This will help answer some of the questions that you have regarding this issue.

Q. Do you have any teachings on "point of contact"? I'd like to show my children how to release their faith, but I don't quite know how to explain it.

A. Oral Roberts is the man who pioneered the concept of "point of contact" faith. I have many teachings on this subject. For example, BULLDOG FAITH is an excellent booklet which contains concise teachings on how to obtain and release faith.

The best way to teach your children faith is to teach them the Word! Because we increase our faith by hearing the Word and release our faith by praying the Word, begin to have them memorize portions of scripture which are promises that cover basic areas and needs in their lives. Teach them that as they speak God's Word, it is powerful and active and will produce results.

A more common point of contact is the prayer cloth which is referred to in Acts 19:12. To release God's anointing into your situation, place an anointed cloth in contact with your need. If you need healing, pin the cloth to your clothing; if your house needs to sell, tape the cloth over the doorpost; or if you have a wayward child, put the cloth in his or her pillowcase.

Q. How can a person do what I Thessalonians 5:17 says and pray without ceasing?

A. Prayer is an intimate conversation with the Father. First Thessalonians 5:17 says to "*Pray without ceasing,*" which reminds us always to be in an attitude of prayer. Whatever we're doing and wherever we are, there should be no time when we are void of the assurance of the presence of God with us and in us. I believe the gift of tongues is such a wonderful channel for praying always and in everything. There is opportunity at all times to be in the Spirit through speaking in tongues.

I learned the importance of praying in tongues while reading the testimony of Dr. Cho. I was convicted when I read how much time he spent in prayer. I remember asking God how could I possibly pray so long when I'm so busy? I was amazed to find out how much time I wasted in a day that could have been used in prayer. Since then, I pray in the Spirit while driving, when studying, etc. Whatever I'm doing, praying only heightens to a greater extent the final product.

Q. Why did David say in the psalms that he prayed against his enemies, but Jesus commands us to pray for our enemies and love them?

A. When David prayed for death and destruction toward his enemies in the psalms, he was not praying against flesh and blood. David was coming against the principalities and powers—the demonic forces—behind the person who was causing him grief: *"For we wrestle not against flesh and blood, but against principalities, against powers, against the rulers of the darkness of this world, against spiritual wickedness in high places"* (Ephesians 6:12). Therefore, it was scriptural for David to pray that the work of his enemies be destroyed, and it was good spiritual warfare to pull down the strongholds that had come against his life.

On the other hand, we are to bless our enemies as Jesus commanded (Luke 6:28) in order that they might come into the knowledge of God and receive Jesus as their personal Lord and Savior. Sometimes I have thought that God allows us to have enemies just so we have the opportunity to bless them, pray for them, and do good to them. Once a man in my city said some very ugly things about me to his congregation. He even called me a false prophetess. Personally, I wanted to tell him off; but the Lord said to me, "How do I treat my enemies?"

I said, "Lord, you love them."

He said, "Treat him the way I would." From that time on whenever I heard that man's name, I said, "Lord, bless him." Then one day God gave me special instructions to bless the man through promoting his church. I obeyed the Lord and saw the fruit of obedience: not long afterward some people from the man's congregation called me saying their pastor's attitude had completely changed. He now spoke highly of me, and he had even invited his congregation to read through the Bible using my monthly devotional plan!

I asked the Lord, "What happened?"

He answered, "When your ways please me, I make even your enemies to be at peace with you."

I don't think you need to speak God's blessings directly to a person who offends you. Sometimes that "enemy" might even be in another state or country, and then you cannot speak to them in person. Bless them in your prayers and pray that God will do good to them. Then if possible, bless them with your actions. Send a letter or some flowers just to say, "I care about you." If you will bless your enemies, pray for them, and do good to them, God will transform those relationships!

Q. Why do we have to pray to the Father in Jesus' name? Can't we call upon Jesus directly? Aren't they one in the same?

A. The reason we need to address the Father in Jesus' name is because Jesus gave us this instruction. He did this because the position of the Father in the Godhead is one of authority.

The Father, Son, and Holy Spirit are three distinct individuals, Who are one in unity. Jesus is not unequal to the Father, but He submits to the Father's authority. A similar illustration would be that a wife is not unequal to her husband, but she is in submission to his headship.

As the architect of the universe, Father God is the One Who has the responsibility to fulfill the prayers we have asked according to His Word. Jesus is our mediator because of His sacrifice; therefore, we come in Jesus' name (see John 16:23).

Q. What is remitting and retaining sins mentioned in John 20:23? Also, please give a clear explanation on binding and loosing in Matthew 18:18.

A. In Matthew 18:18 it says that whatever we bind on earth is bound in heaven and whatever we loose on earth is loosed in heaven. This means that, first of all, our binding and our loosing must agree with heavenly principles of the kingdom. When we bind something, the Greek infers that it is already bound in heaven; and when we loose something, it's already loosed in heaven. We have the authority to bind those things which heaven binds, and the authority to loose those things which heaven looses.

According to other scriptures, we have the power to bind the strong man, Satan, and to ''spoil his household''; but in the context of Matthew 18:18, it suggests that if we loose a person from their sins—if we forgive their offenses—then we are free and that person is free. If we are unwilling to forgive, we have not only bound the person we don't forgive but we bind ourselves as well. John 20:23 is a restatement of this principle.

In a broader meaning also, we are given authority and power in Jesus' name to bind evil and the work of Satan. We can also loose the Holy Spirit and loose ourselves from Satan's power.

Q. What does the writer of James mean when he mentions ''praying amiss?''

A. Asking amiss is defined by James as a prayer which satisfies our own worldly lusts (see James 4). This chapter also discusses other reasons for unanswered prayer: lust, murders, covetousness, strife, adulteries, pride, rebellion against God, backsliding, sin, and doublemindedness.

Any prayer that is prayed according to the promises of God will never be "amiss" (I John 5:14,15).

Q. Is it scriptural to plead the blood for needs other than salvation, such as safety in travel or protection for our home?

A. "Pleading the blood" refers to our covenant cut by Jesus who shed His blood for the remission of our sins. You can certainly plead the blood over everything you have. The Israelites put blood on their doorposts which protected their homes and possessions as well as the people within them. You can do the same in your personal life as well.

The way you plead the blood of Jesus is simply to speak the words, "I plead the blood of Jesus over (name the person, place, or situation)." According to Psalms 91:11 the Father gives the angels charge to do the specific work which you desire.

The power of Christ's blood shed on Calvary is what overcomes Satan's work (see I John 3:8). That same blood protects the believer and reminds Satan's hosts that you believe in the sacrifice of Christ and accept the divine work of the Crucifixion and Resurrection. The Resurrection is the seal of the power of the blood, which is like a supernatural covering or armor for the believer. Because Satan cannot penetrate through this armor once it is invoked by the believer, the blood of Christ is the most important protection a believer has (see Revelation 12:11).

Q. What are the spiritual benefits of fasting, and how should you prepare to go on a fast? How do you know if the Lord is directing you to do so?

A. By studying Joel 2 and Isaiah 58, you can get a good idea of what fasting will do for you. Matthew 17:21 connects prayer and fasting with overcoming disbelief or, in other words, feeding your faith and starving your doubts.

Jesus was spiritually prepared before the Holy Spirit led Him to fast for 40 days (see Matthew 4:1). If you are going to fast or if you sense in your spirit that God is calling you to a fast, seek Him in prayer for specific direction. The Spirit's leading is a still small voice within your spirit and is also known as an "inner witness" (see I Kings 19:12). I wouldn't suggest that you be like Moses and fast for 40 days because it could be very dangerous. Instead, be led of the Spirit in your fasting; and let the Lord lead you in setting up a time frame.

There are many good books dealing with this subject. Because the material is so voluminous, I would encourage you to go to a Christian bookstore and buy resource materials on the benefits of and preparation for fasting.

Q. How long should I fast?

A. If you have never learned to fast, I suggest that you begin by fasting one meal. My husband, who had never been taught fasting when he first began to serve the Lord, was very concerned about a friend of his who was in a mental ward. As he prayed for his friend, the Lord spoke to him out of Matthew 17:21. He didn't know anything about fasting—or how long to fast—so he fasted one meal. Even after such a short fast, the man was released from the hospital!

If you are having trouble fasting an entire meal, then try drinking juice or simply fasting desserts. As you get victory in this area, then you can begin to fast more meals at one time. The key is consistency, not duration. Another important point to remember is to keep God's twins of fasting and prayer together, and you will have the most effective prayer life you have ever had!

Q. Jesus said that the bride does not fast while the bridegroom is with her (see Mark 2:19). Jesus is fully with us isn't He? Why do you encourage the fast?

A. Mark 2:19 and Matthew 9:15 speak of the bridegroom and fasting. Notice in Matthew 9:15 it says, ". . . *but the days will come, when the bridegroom shall be taken from them, and then shall they fast.*" Jesus said in John 15 that He would be taken away and it was to our advantage that He go away since He would send the Helper, the Holy Spirit, Who would be with us. Technically speaking it is not Jesus in the fullness of His Being Who is with us, rather it is the Holy Spirit Who indwells us.

Chapter Eleven

PERSONAL APPEARANCE AND CHARACTER

Q. I have been having a difficult time getting 40 hours a week in at work because I can't get my mind off God and all the things I need to do to be a good witness for Him. I know God doesn't want me to be a thief and steal from my employer; yet, when an opportunity arises to witness to someone or comfort someone at work, I just have to put that first. Do you have any suggestions?

A. Although it is a temptation to witness to or comfort someone at work, it is important that we realize that by doing so we *are* stealing from our employer. God does not want us to steal from a human agency in order to give time to Him—this goes against all of His principles and laws. Let me suggest that you do these things during your lunch hour, on breaks, after work, or on weekends.

If you're being paid to work 40 hours a week, then according to God's laws, you must work 40 hours per week. This will positively affect your boss' attitude toward you and even will be influential in consideration for raises, promotions, etc. God wants us to be people of excellence on our jobs—our actions are a better witness than our words can ever be!

I encourage you to stick with the policies of your company and be honest! The Lord will honor your faithfulness to your company and return that to you in other ways. Give your company your very best, and God will give you the very best (II Corinthians 9:6).

Q. Just what is classified as gossiping, and is it always negative?

A. Although the King James Version does not use the word gossip, we find similar words that mean the same thing. *Backbiting* means talebearing or gossiping (Psalms 15:3; Proverbs 25:23; II Corinthians 12:20). It can also refer to slander; it is always used in a negative sense. In the Greek *backbiting* means "evil speaking,'' whereas the Hebrew meaning is, again, a reference to a talebearer or someone who brings something negative concerning another person.

Q. What is the dividing line or the difference between living like a Christian and being a doormat for others? Jesus said to turn the other cheek and not to turn away borrowers, but where is the balance?

A. When Jesus told Christians to turn the other cheek (Matthew 5:39), He was not talking about being a doormat and taking all kinds of bad treatment. He simply meant not to return evil with evil, but rather to treat others with love and compassion. He did not, however, want us to contribute to their delinquency or to allow them to continue in their evil ways.

Q. Recently I was joking with my mother, and my little brother turned around and said I had lied. My mother and I could plainly see it wasn't true—it was just a joke. Is it wrong to joke?

A. Because I do not know all the details, it would be difficult for me to determine whether your ''joke'' was a ''lie.'' The Lord wants us to have a good time and to laugh and have fun, but not at the expense of perverse speech.

Jesus warned us about the importance of our words: *''But I say unto you, That every idle word that men shall speak, they shall give account thereof in the day of judgment''* (Matthew 12:36). The word *idle* means ''barren, slow, inactive, or useless.'' By all means the Lord wants you to continue having fun, but be careful what direction that fun takes. Life and death are in the power of the tongue, and we must be very careful in the things that we speak if we are to mature and grow in the Lord (Proverbs 18:21).

Something you need to consider when you are having ''fun''

is the motive behind the things you say—the outcome of such comments can be devastating. A person who purposely deceives his neighbor, slandering him while pretending it is all a joke, is compared in scripture to a mad man who casts fiery darts, arrows, and death (Proverbs 26:18,19).

Q. I am a secretary, and I get ten sick days a year. What do I do when I've used up all my personal and vacation time, and I am not sick but want to use a sick day?

A. The reason employees are given sick days is for those emergency situations when an employee actually needs them. If you have sick days coming and have not used them, then praise God that He has given you health! Employers consider those employees who have not used up their sick time a valuable asset. This even may be a part of your evaluation when you are considered for a raise and receive your personnel review.

If you are not sick, it is dishonest to use that time as sick time. If you need a personal day off, then go to your supervisor and ask what the company policy is on using sick days for personal time. Take Peter's advice and lay aside all guile, that is dishonesty (I Peter 2:2).

Q. I need specific steps to overcome distraction and disobedience. I have found that many times I have been distracted or sidetracked from tasks and then found myself in disorder because I hadn't done what I was supposed to do. Can you help me in this area?

A: Psalms 90:12 says, "*So teach us to number our days, that we may apply our hearts unto wisdom.*" In this context, the word *number* means "to organize." The psalmist was saying, "teach us to organize our activities so that our days will be filled with wisdom."

Begin each day with prayer and study in God's Word. Jesus

never lost sight of His goals, because they were centered on God's Word. With the Word and fellowship with God as your first priority, you will bring the supernatural into your activities.

Make a daily list of what you need to achieve. This will make your goals tangible and easier to accomplish and will help you organize the best plan for getting things done in the right order. Also develop a weekly activity schedule—long-range planning is as vital as short- range planning—and assign all of your activities to the day in which they are to be accomplished.

Remember to schedule time for problems or interruptions. That way, if something unexpected comes up, your schedule is still preserved. Follow through with these four rules for successful organization of time, and don't let your emotions dictate your activities. Keep your eyes on the goal and be committed to accomplishing them; then let the Holy Spirit redeem your time and make every day the best day of your life (see Ephesians 5:16).

Q. One day you read from Genesis 35:4 and said that earrings have some idolatrous meaning. Where is that found in the Bible? And is it OK if I have my ears pierced?

A. In preparation for returning to the land of his inheritance, Jacob commanded all who were with him to put away the strange gods that were among them in Genesis 35:2. They obeyed his command in verse 4 by giving him the strange gods in their hands and their earrings. God does not forbid the use of earrings if they aren't idolatrous in nature. (See Genesis 24:22 and Ezekiel 16:12.)

As far as pierced ears are concerned, God commanded the Israelites of the Old Testament not to cut or mark their bodies because the heathen people around them did these things as a part of their pagan worship. In some cases it was a form of self abasement to achieve holiness; in other cases, it identified their relationship to their demon gods.

Piercing ears in order to wear earrings is neither for the purpose of affliction nor identification. First Peter 3:3-5 tells us not to let our adornment be external ONLY. Scripture does not say NOT to wear makeup, perfume, etc.; it simply tells us not to depend upon outward appearance, because God wants us beautiful on the inside as well. So these things are perfectly fine to use if done tastefully. Scripture does not prohibit us from "adorning" ourselves in order to make us look more attractive; so be at peace regarding your pierced ears and your earrings.

Q. Is it OK to use makeup? Is it scriptural?

A. Scripture doesn't tell us what kind of makeup women in the Bible used, but we do know from historical records that they used such things as ointment, perfume, henna, rouge, and powder. Job had a beautiful daughter named *Keren-happuch*, which means "horn of the cosmetic." Evidently she had beautiful eyes, and possibly wore color to keep them beautiful. I don't think there is anything wrong with using makeup to cover up some of our bad points and highlight our good ones.

Q. How can a Christian couple have a pure, Christian dating experience? Are touching and kissing taboo?

A. I believe the most precious gift a Christian couple can have while dating is to receive the covering and protection of God over their relationship. Putting your relationship in the hands of God means trusting Him in everything. He will remind you to pray for and over the time you spend together. Pray that you will keep your minds renewed on spiritual and not fleshly thoughts (Philippians 4:8; Romans 12:1,2). God is your ultimate protection. He did away with the flesh and exalted the Spirit through Christ Jesus (Romans 8:2; II Thessalonians 3:3).

Do touching, holding hands, hugging, and kissing keep you away from a godly walk? Anything that we let have dominion over us will control us (Romans 6:16). Give God dominion—He is bigger than any stumbling block that Satan may attempt to put in your way. Commit your ways to Him, and you can have a godly dating relationship.

Q. I am a single Christian lady, and I want a mate. Should I entrust this to God or should I initiate interest?

A. Here is a simple Bible formula for God's perfect plan for your life: put God and His plan for you first—not your desire for marriage (Matthew 6:33). Don't let the enemy make you anxious about choosing. Remember Satan *drives* the sheep; but Jesus leads them.

I have a tape series entitled "Your Right Mate," that will help you understand God's will for marriage. Also, here are some scriptures you might want to use in praying for a mate: Isaiah 62:5, Ephesians 5:28, and James 3:17.

I believe that there is nothing wrong with making a list of the qualities that you would desire in your future mate. According to Mark 11:23,24 the prayer of faith requires that we be specific in our requests. God has many desires and plans for our life including a mate; but until we ask for them, He cannot move to bring these things forth in our lives. So by all means pray for the very specific qualities you would desire, and enjoy this time with the Lord.

Q. I have had a life-long problem with pride. The Bible says "humble yourself." Can you tell me how to do this?

A. The way we humble ourselves is very simple. To be "humble" means to submit to God and to what His Word tells us to do. Jesus is our example of this. Philippians 2:5-8 tells us He died to His own earthly desires and became completely submissive to the will of God. Although Jesus was equal with God, the Bible tells us that He did not regard His equality with God as a thing to hang onto, but He humbled Himself and became obedient unto death on the Cross. Jesus died as a lowly servant.

To humble yourself does NOT mean abasement or "lily-livered behavior." It is simply agreeing with what God's Word says about you. God never whips us into submission. He causes us to be teachable by drawing us with His love.

Q. My husband does not want to attend church with me, nor does he approve of the church I attend. What should I do?

A. When my mother faced the same problem that you face—my father did not want to go to church with her and didn't like the church that she attended—she assured him that she would go to his church Sunday mornings if she could go to her choice on Sunday and Wednesday nights. She also assured him that she would be the very best wife to him—she would fix better meals, keep a cleaner house, and love him more—and she proved that by her actions. At first he didn't like her church (neither did my brother nor I); but in time we were all born again and Spirit-filled in that church.

I would encourage you to attend church for regular services—don't compromise—and to assure your husband that you will be a better wife. As you show him love by your actions, I believe you will win him to the Lord.

The Bible instructs wives, whose husbands are disobedient to the Word, to win them without a word by their chaste and respectful behavior toward them. (See I Peter 3:1.) To "win without a word" means **don't nag!** Proverbs says that a wise woman builds her house, but the foolish one tears it down with her own hands. We need to build up our husbands, instead of tearing them down by our nagging and criticism.

Q. Is it right for a woman who is filled with the Holy Ghost to wear slacks?

A. Deuteronomy 22:5 says, *"The woman shall not wear that which pertaineth unto a man, neither shall a man put on a woman's garment: for all that do so are abomination unto the LORD thy God."*

Very clearly this scripture says that a woman shall not wear a man's clothing, and a man shall not wear a woman's clothing. Women's slacks—slacks which are tailored and designed specifically for women—are not a man's clothing. Slacks are appropriate in certain cultures according to the custom of that society. In our society it is perfectly acceptable for a woman to wear women's slacks.

Q. Why don't women keep their heads covered in church anymore?

A. Paul discussed head coverings for women in I Corinthians 11. In the age in which Paul lived, it was customary for a married woman to wear a head covering. This symbolized that she was married, belonged to a man, and submitted to his authority. Just as it would be regarded disrespectful in this society for a man to wear a hat in church, so it was disrespectful for a married woman not to wear a covering. Women without coverings over their head were considered prostitutes.

I personally believe the issue that hair is a covering relates to the culture of the day. A chaste woman of Paul's day (Christian or otherwise) wore her hair longer than a man because it was a disgrace for her to be uncovered in public. Paul is admonishing the Christian woman to be an example to other women. We find a similar situation in the matter of eating meat offered to idols. Today we do not deal with such issues in our culture, but it was an important matter to the first-century Christians. Paul said he knew that in Christ he had perfect liberty; but for the sake of others, he would do nothing to cause them to stumble. He advised the Church to live in like manner (Romans 14:12,13; I Corinthians 8:9).

Q. Is it wrong for a woman or a man to dye their gray hair? I am 29 years old, and my gray hair does not look good on me. I've been told that I'll be missing God's best if I color my hair because Proverbs says that gray hair is the splendor of the old.

A. It is true that Proverbs 20:29 says that gray hair is the "*. . . beauty of old men . . .*"; however, you hardly qualify as "old"! I see nothing wrong with an individual covering prematurely gray hair.

Q. I've heard you say that women should dress modestly. Recently I purchased a suede miniskirt that is approximately four inches above the knee. Do you think it is okay to wear it?

A. I personally do not consider miniskirts to be truly modest apparel for a Christian woman. However, age, size, and the occasion for such dress all play a part in the decision. Shorts, for example, may be all right for a picnic or the beach but wholly out of order for the office or church. Use good taste in choosing your clothing.

Believers should love the Lord and His Church enough to care about the image they are portraying and the testimony they leave with the world. The apostle Paul said that all things are lawful but not all things are expedient (I Corinthians 10:23), and he warned against causing a brother to stumble (Romans 14:21).

Chapter Twelve

FEELINGS AND ATTITUDES

Q. I'm a Vietnam veteran and am having financial problems. I'm so glad that Jesus treats me better than the government does.

A. I sense that you are hurt over your experience in Vietnam. I am glad that you are able to turn to Jesus whenever you feel overwhelmed. Jesus is truly the ". . . *friend that sticketh closer than a brother*" (Proverbs 18:24).

Ask the Holy Spirit to reveal any bitterness resulting from past hurts. Hebrews 12:15 says that bitterness can spring up and defile you. By faith, forgive every person you know who has wounded you and get free from bitterness. If we hold unforgiveness in our hearts, not only will it result in bitterness but it will also give permission for Satan to send tormenters to torment us (Matthew 18:21-35).

Although many people have found it hard to forgive those who have hurt them deeply, I remind them that Jesus forgave us even though we did not deserve nor earn forgiveness from Him. But out of His great love with which He loved us, He released forgiveness to us. In His strength and ability, we can release forgiveness to others.

Q. What are "soul ties," and how do they hinder the Christian walk?

A. A soul tie, or bonding between two individuals, may be formed by shared experiences or by similar mental likes and dislikes. Some people in the New Age Movement use this term, and there may be many different definitions possible. In our Christian walk a soul tie may simply be the strong affection that links a mother and her children. This type of bond may hinder a parent-child relationship if the mother is unwilling to "release" her child to develop adult skills and responsibilities. The mother may also become so bound up in her child's life that all her waking hours are spent in fear and worry over what the child is doing while away from home. Emotional dependency of this kind is not good. We must always be dependent on the Lord.

Soul ties can also be formed through sexual relationships. The Scripture warns that this type of bond outside of the marriage union is a sin against your own body and literally defiles the temple of God (I Corinthians 6:15-20).

Q. I am a housewife with small children, and I get depressed and tired. Can you give me any advice for my situation?

A. I can really understand your feelings of depression. When my children were young I would get depressed (tiredness and passivity is a sign of depression). My husband would say, "Sing a song!"

I'd tell him I didn't feel like singing and to leave me alone, but he wouldn't quit until I would sing with him. Lo and behold, it was singing in the midst of a storm that would fill my inner being with peace and rest. As I focused upon praising God, the REAL me—in Christ—would shine through. So my first advice is to sing praises.

Next, set a schedule for yourself: (1) start your day with prayer and the study of God's Word; (2) make a daily list of what you need to achieve, then follow your list; and (3) remember to schedule time for problems or interruptions by the children. That way if something unexpected comes up, your schedule is still preserved.

The more time you spend in fellowshiping with Jesus and studying His Word, the more energy you will have. As you feed your spirit and pray, you will find energy flowing into your body: *"But they that wait upon the LORD shall renew their strength; they shall mount up with wings as eagles; they shall run, and not be weary; and they shall walk, and not faint"* (Isaiah 40:31).

Q. Where is the line between murmuring, which is displeasing to God, and asking, which is our God-given privilege?

A. The fine line between murmuring and asking is an attitude of the heart. God desires to give us answers to our questions, and these answers will always be in line with His Word. Murmuring is complaining! When we murmur and complain, we reveal a lack of gratitude and faith in God to change circumstances or to provide what is needed (Exodus 14:10-14). Murmuring is a very serious sin which opens us up to satanic attack (Numbers 11:1; Psalms 77:3; I Corinthians 10:10).

Q. I have an overwhelming problem with jealousy. It is so ugly, and it is practically killing me. Can you help me conquer this?

A. The Bible says that jealousy is as cruel as the grave (Song of Solomon 8:6). Jealousy motivates revenge and can cause you many problems unless you repent. The only way you can overcome jealousy is to go to God and ask Him to help you with your problem. God guarantees in His Word that if we resist the devil he will have to flee (James 4:7). As you feel this spirit of jealousy trying to overtake you, speak out loud, ''Jealousy, I resist you in Jesus' name.'' Remember the root of jealousy is fear, and perfect love casts out fear (I John 4:18).

Q. I have heard you say we are not to take up another's offense. Is there a scripture reference to support this statement?

A. Proverbs 26:17 gives us advice about keeping out of someone else's quarrel. In the Amplified Bible it reads, *''He who, passing by, stops to meddle with strife that is not his business is like one who takes a dog by the ears.''*

Q. Is it ever proper to judge someone?

A. I encourage everyone in the Body of Christ to look at others as having the potential of Jesus inside. There is no proper or improper time to judge another. The Bible tells us that such behavior will get us into a world of trouble. The consequences of judging are found in Matthew 7:1-5; Romans 2:1; and Galatians 6:7,8.

God will help us love others in the Church, and through that love we won't have to judge or evaluate them. After all, we are God's servants and it is God alone who is able to make us stand (see Romans 14:4). Each of us is to evaluate and judge ourselves—then we will not need to judge one another.

Q. Marilyn, I am a prisoner of agoraphobia—a fear of open spaces. I have had this all my life, but only recently have found there is a name for it. I am a born-again, Spirit-filled Christian. Is there help for me?

A. First of all, recognize that you are battling a spirit of fear and it does not come from God (II Timothy 1:7). Your major weapon against this spirit is the Word of God. You can start by putting on the full armor of God found in Ephesians 6. Do this by speaking the Word, and visualizing the armor covering, surrounding, and protecting you. As you carry the armor of God into open spaces, you will not actually be in the open, but in your armor!

Jesus once said that this kind of spirit can't be eradicated except through fasting and prayer. So bathe this situation in prayer and much fasting. Also visualize yourself hidden in Christ as Colossians 3:3 says. Meditate upon this scripture until it becomes real to you, and then command the spirit of fear to leave your life in the name of Jesus and not to harass you any more.

I would encourage you to find a Spirit-filled Christian counselor. I believe it would be helpful to you to have a Christian who can encourage you and pray for you, so that you can be delivered from this thing. Remember, Jesus came to set the captives free!

Q. How do you "seek first the kingdom"? Some people say to keep your eyes on Jesus but I'm not sure I know what that means. Secondly, how do I acknowledge God in all my ways?

A. The scripture you are referring to is found in Matthew 6:33. To "seek first the kingdom of God" refers to putting God first in everything we do. We are to make Him number one in our lives; our desire to please Him should be greater than life itself. We put Him first when we do what He instructs us to do in His Word. And by doing this, we are acknowledging Who God is and freeing Him to direct our paths (Proverbs 3:6).

Q. How are Christians the salt of the earth?

A. Salt contains three qualities: it preserves or purifies, it seasons, and it causes one to be thirsty. As Christians we are to do all three of these things if we are to be the salt of the earth. It is the light of our testimony and our holy walk with the Lord which will preserve and sanctify the cities and nations in which we live. Jesus in a Christian's life makes life worth living. We are seasoning—and Jesus is our "spice of life!" It is our relationship with the Lord which will cause others to be thirsty for the "living water"—Jesus Christ.

Q. I have a neighbor who wanders through my house without my permission, goes through my mail, etc. Can you give me some suggestions on how to handle her?

A. No one has the right to enter another person's home or go through another's things without permission. You need to confront your neighbor and put a stop to such behavior. Be firm as well as loving, and let her know you mean what you say. Don't concern yourself about whether or not this will end your relationship with your neighbor. You will still be right in ending rude and presumptuous behavior, and you will be doing your neighbor a service.

Q. I am a diesel mechanic and work with some rough men. My problem is the music they listen to is hard rock and it is loud. I've asked them to turn it down; I have even gone to the foreman and the management, but they won't turn it down. What should I do?

A. I suggest you purchase a small headset radio and play Christian music while you work. This will eliminate you having to hear the rock music, it will keep you at peace, and will keep your mind on Jesus (see Isaiah 26:3).

I would also encourage you to begin claiming favor from God and man (see Psalms 5:12). How do you do this? By confessing the Word of God over your situation. God's supernatural favor with the people on your job will turn this situation around.

Q. What does righteous indignation mean?

A. Most people think of righteous indignation as having a sense of justified anger. There are certain ungodly situations where it is perfectly acceptable to be angry over an unjust circumstance. The Bible says to be angry but not to sin and to deal with each situation immediately so that no bitter roots will take hold in our lives (see Ephesians 4:26; Hebrews 12:15).

Q. Where did the races come from?

A. The different breakdown of ethnic groups can be found in Genesis 9-11. Scripture tells us that all mankind is derived from

Noah and his sons Shem, Ham, and Japheth. Both biblical and historical documents indicate that Shem is the ancestral father of the Jewish and Arab nations; Blacks, Mongoloids, and Indians descended from the loins of Ham; and Japheth fathered the Caucasian race.

Q. My husband is very critical of me. Whenever I witness to anyone about Jesus, he criticizes the way I do it. If I tell him about how I taught my Sunday school class, he always tells me the wrong things I've done. Occasionally I solo in our church, and he is even critical of the way I stand. I am tired of this. What can I do?

A. Many times the criticisms of our mates toward us can be the most piercing of all. Some years ago I experienced very much what you are experiencing. My husband's criticism hurt me so much that I never wanted him to be in a room where I was teaching because he always told me all the negative things I had done. It seemed I could take criticism from anyone but him. The Lord began to deal with me and show me that what I was receiving was what I had sown.

My husband is a pastor. And the Lord spoke to me and said, "What do you say to him about his sermons?"

I began to think about some of my comments, and they weren't always so good. From that day on I promised the Lord that I would look at all the good things that my husband spoke and all the good things he did in the ministry; and that's exactly what I began to do. And you know, the more I complimented my husband, the more I saw his preaching and teaching improve.

Do you know what began to happen in return? My husband began complimenting me! If you want to reap good, positive, and helpful things from your husband, then sow those things into his life. We reap what we sow. We need to look at what we're sowing when the harvest isn't what we'd like it to be.

Q. Do you think that a married person flirting with the opposite sex is healthy if it is done in the "right perspective"? I'm personally jealous of my husband when he does this. Am I being too insecure?

A. I do not believe it is ever "healthy" to flirt with the opposite sex. There is no such thing as a "right perspective" in this. Flirting with the opposite sex is flirting with disaster or playing with the teeth of a lion when the lion's mouth is open.

Your jealousy is not good either. There's no reason why your husband can't speak to other women. If this is all he is doing, then there is no need for your jealousy. But if your husband is actually flirting, I suggest you have a heart-to-heart talk with him, and tell him how you feel. If he is unresponsive, then begin praying that God will give him wisdom and reveal your heart to him. In the meantime give your husband all the love and affection that he needs and assure him that he has first place in your life.

Q. I have a real hard time forgiving myself when I've offended someone or done something stupid. What should I do?

A. Peter, Paul, David, Abraham, and Isaac all sinned. The key to their success and greatness was that they received forgiveness and cleansing from their sin and went on with God. Realize that you are not perfect but you do have the perfect One living inside of you. Whenever you feel you've blown it, repent to God and to anyone else who may be involved. Then forgive yourself and thank God that you are in Christ and no longer under condemnation (Romans 8:1,2). His Word is true and He forgives every repentant sinner according to I John 1:9.

Q. Marilyn, I have been deeply hurt by people telling lies about me. How do I handle this kind of gossip?

A. First of all, you must guard your own heart according to Proverbs 4:23. I was once deeply offended by another Christian. I felt that he was being very unjust toward me, and my first reaction was to tell him off; but the Holy Spirit whispered to my heart to do good to those who hate me (Matthew 5:44). I made a decision to act on the Word, to pray for the person who offended me, and to do good for him if the opportunity arose.

Likewise it is important for you to forgive the people who are gossiping about you and to make sure that your relationship with the Lord continues to be good. As you walk in holiness and righteousness before Him, God will make your enemies to be at peace with you (Proverbs 16:7). If you sow bitterness, you will reap bitter results; but God will richly bless you if you flow in His forgiveness and grace toward these people.

Q. Is it possible to forgive but still prosecute, or should we forgive and let the person go free?

A. It is possible to forgive a person and still prosecute him because, in certain cases, this too can be an act of love. If the person who has offended you or violated your legal rights is a Christian, then the Word of God has an answer for you. The guideline for which action to follow is found in Matthew 18:15-17.

You must follow the leading of the Holy Spirit on whether or not to confront a person with an offense they have caused you. If the offense took place a long time ago and the Holy Spirit continues to deal with you even though you have totally forgiven the person of the offense, you must be obedient to the Holy Spirit.

Most often the Lord will allow us to forgive a person, and then instruct us to leave these things in our past and go on. To bring up these unknown offenses may only cause further strife. There may be a time when the Holy Spirit will direct us to confront a brother or sister in the Lord in order to prevent them from causing a similar offense in a repeated manner. Again, you must follow the leading of the Spirit.

Chapter Thirteen
CHRISTIAN CITIZENSHIP

Q. Please give me scripture that tells me why abortion is wrong.

A. Before I answer your question, let me address another point. Despite the horror associated with the murder of so many innocent babies, God can forgive any woman who has had an abortion. In fact, anyone who is responsible for abortions—from the parents to the doctors to the legislators—can repent right now and be forgiven by God.

God sees our substance—all that we are and ever will be—while we are yet unborn! God creates and calls forth life. Who is man to determine whether an unborn child has the "right" to live or die? To abort a child is to deny that it is an individual separate from the mother. If a mother wants a child, she calls it "a baby." But if the child is unwanted, she calls it "a fetus." But whatever you call it, that child was made by God: *"Did not he that made me in the womb make him? and did not one fashion us in the womb?"* (Job 31:15).

Exodus 20:13 says, *"Thou shalt not kill"*; the word *kill* means "murder." When abortion takes place, murder takes place. Every day in hospitals, doctors' offices, and clinics, babies are being murdered. Many of those babies are so developed that they could have lived.

Not only does Scripture tell us that God made us, it offers more than enough proof that unborn babies have complete personalities. Psalms 139:14-18 tells us that at the moment of conception—perhaps even earlier—the tiny child's personality begins forming: *"I will praise thee; for I am fearfully and wonderfully made: marvellous are thy works; and that my soul knoweth right well. My substance was not hid from thee, when I was made in secret, and curiously wrought in the lowest parts of the earth. Thine eyes did see my substance, yet being unperfect; and in thy book all my members were written, which in continuance were fashioned, when as yet there was none of them. How precious also are thy thoughts unto me, O God! how great is the sum of them! If I should count them, they are more in number than the sand: when I awake, I am still with thee.*"

Psalms 22:9,10 says, "*But thou art he that took me out of the womb: thou didst make me hope when I was upon my mother's breasts. I was cast upon thee from the womb: thou art my God from my mother's belly.*" The psalmist is saying, "Even before my birth, You were my God."

Isaiah 44:2 says, "*Thus saith the LORD that made thee, and formed thee from the womb, ...*" Throughout the Bible God emphasizes the value of life in the mother's womb. He even revealed the personalities of certain people before they were born!

Jacob and Esau were both known by God before their births. God also told Jeremiah, "*Before I formed thee in the belly I knew thee; and before thou camest forth out of the womb I sanctified thee, and I ordained thee a prophet unto the nations*" (Jeremiah 1:5).

God named seven people in the Bible before their births, and several of them were named before conception! They were Ishmael (Genesis 16:11), Isaac (Genesis 17:19), Josiah (I Kings 13:2), Solomon (I Chronicles 22:9), Cyrus (Isaiah 44:28;45:1), John the Baptist (Luke 1:13), and Jesus (Matthew 1:21).

It is my firm belief that the crime of abortion has brought a curse upon this country. If you have had an abortion, take a moment right now to repent of your sin. Ask God's forgiveness and He will give it to you. Then what better step can you take than to help others learn the truth about abortion?

Q. Should believers take part in the demonstrations going on in front of abortion clinics? I found a scripture that really hit me: "*If thou forbear to deliver them that are drawn unto death, and those that are ready to be slain; If thou sayest, Behold, we knew it not; doth not he that pondereth the heart consider it? and he that keepeth thy soul, doth not he know it? and shall not he render to every man according to his works?*" (Proverbs 24:11,12).

A. Each individual must do as the Holy Spirit leads him/her. I believe Christians have an obligation to become involved in stopping the murder of innocent children, and that may include participation in public demonstrations. Proverbs 24:11,12 could certainly refer to abortion clinics.

Christians must take a stand against abortion: *"Open thy mouth for the dumb in the cause of all such as are appointed to destruction"* (Proverbs 31:8). There can be no such thing as a "neutral" or "uninvolved" stand in the life of a Christian. The unborn cannot open their mouths to cry out for justice against the stealing of lives. But we can cry out for them. Write to your senator and representative, and get as involved as possible with the measures it takes to rid our country of abortion. We dare not stand aside and do nothing: "*. . . Inasmuch as ye have done it unto one of the least of these my brethren, ye have done it unto me*" (Matthew 25:40).

Q. Is the death penalty (capital punishment) all right for today?

A. Numbers 35 gives our governments clear instruction regarding the death penalty. It is valid for today as is every part of the Word of God because God's Word is the same yesterday, today, and forever.

Q. Deuteronomy 13 tells us that false prophets and idolaters should be killed. Yet this exhortation was given after the Ten Commandments were given. Does this not directly contradict the sixth commandment? Also is it of any significance in Deuteronomy 13 that parents are not mentioned?

A. The sixth commandment is a law against the murder of innocent people—it does not contradict the punishment by death of those who commit certain crimes. This distinction is made throughout the Old Testament. So the reference in Deuteronomy 13 to killing false prophets and idolaters is consistent with the sixth commandment which says, "Do not murder."

I believe the absence of "mother and father" in the list of those to be killed (Deuteronomy 13:6) means that children (adult or otherwise) were not to be the ones to kill their parents—the verse says that spouses were responsible for their partners, not the children of that person.

Q. Should we as believers obey all laws over us?

A. First Peter 2:13,15 says, "*Submit yourselves to every ordinance of man for the Lord's sake: . . . For so is the will of God, that with well doing ye may put to silence the ignorance of foolish men.*" God does not violate His own commands. He set up governments for the sake of law and order, and we are required to submit to that law.

Q. I can't believe that God would ever place evil, ungodly men in government positions, yet Romans 13 seems to make this implication. Please help me understand this.

A. Though God does establish governments, He does not appoint evil rulers and authorities. Romans 13 is referring to authority as a general principle—not as a specific person; so you see these verses are not talking about particular individuals being established in government.

God is a God of order, and that's why He set up authorities to rule and keep peace in any given civilization. These people are put there by an act of the *will of man*—not God. God will not violate the free will of man; so if man chooses to put wicked people into office or wicked people force their way into a position of authority, God will not violate the free will of man. Therefore, we cannot assume that it is His perfect will for certain people to be in positions of authority.

If someone in authority over us asks us to do something against God or the direction of His Word, then according to Acts 4:19, we must obey God above man's authority. And if the governing authority is abusive, we have a God who will deal with that authority when we appeal to Him in prayer. It may also be necessary to seek legal recourse through local, state, or federal courts.

Q. One of our church members is having his wages garnisheed by the IRS because he refuses to pay taxes. What does the Bible have to say about taxes?

A. When Jesus was challenged by the Pharisees as to whether or not they should pay taxes to Caesar, Jesus answered with "*. . . Render to Caesar the things that are Caesar's, and to God the things that are God's . . .*" (Mark 12:17).

Matthew 17:24-27 records the incident when tax collectors came to Jesus and asked Him to pay His taxes. Jesus sent Peter to catch a fish; and when Peter opened the fish's mouth, the money for their taxes was inside! So Jesus paid taxes, and taught us that we should also.

Romans 13:1 tells us to submit to our governing authorities. It is our responsibility as American citizens to pay our taxes. Even though taxes may seem extremely high, it is still our duty to pay them. The balance in this teaching is that we also must be good stewards of the financial increase God gives us. Christians can and should take the legal deductions that belong to us—but by all means, scripturally we must pay our taxes.

If you believe your tax assessments are wrong, work for and vote for the candidates who will work to cut government spending.

Q. Is it a sin not to vote? Does it mean you are disobeying God? I was told religion and politics don't mix.

A. God certainly mixed religion and politics. It is God's desire to have godly governments which rule under His laws and with His Holy Spirit guiding and leading: *"When the righteous are in authority, the people rejoice: but when the wicked beareth rule, the people mourn"* (Proverbs 29:2). Although it is not a sin to refrain from voting, I believe it is a *Christian's responsibility* to vote in order to make sure that godly Christian men and women are put into office.

Q. Wasn't smuggling Bibles into China a dishonest thing to do?

A. In Acts 4:19 the "government" told the apostles not to speak of Jesus, but they disobeyed the "official" law of man in order to obey God. Jesus specifically told us to "*. . . Go ye into all the world, and preach the gospel to every creature*" (Mark 16:15). "All the world" includes China. We are obeying God when we take Bibles to people deprived of the Word of God due to the will of men. It is not illegal for *us* to take in the Bibles; but it is illegal for the *Chinese* to have Bibles. When non-Chinese are found with Bibles, the Chinese officials just take the Bibles and issue a receipt which allows the Bibles to be retrieved when one leaves China.

Q. What does the Bible say about unions, striking, and everything that goes along with it?

A. The Bible is silent about our modern-day unions. The matter of unions and striking is between you and the Lord. So long as you are not engaging in any illegal acts, the best course of action would be to pray and let the peace of God guide your decisions (see Colossians 3:15).

Q. I have been a police officer for six years. How can I be a true Christian with a job like mine? Sometimes I have to lie to get people to do what I want them to do.

A. I believe that it is always possible to be a police officer and still maintain your Christian principles. I feel that as you pray for wisdom, God will give you words to speak in truth, which will still bring the desired results you need in your work. Begin to claim the wisdom that the Scriptures promise you (see I Corinthians 1:30; Ephesians 1:17; and James 1:5).

As you pray for wisdom in what you do and say, God will begin to give you creative alternatives and ideas from His very own wisdom! You will find that there are always ways to remain committed and yet maintain your moral standards. Because your job is so involved and complicated, I feel the James 1:5 prayer is your greatest weapon—go for it! You will be a blessing to your police force and a blessing to those people you serve and protect in your community.

Q. I know the Bible says that we should not be unequally yoked. Does this just apply to marriage or does it apply to business as well? I own and operate my own business and a non-Christian is interested in joining me in partnership. Also, should I restrict my dealings to other Christian businesses?

A. The Bible says not to be unequally yoked, so I don't believe Christians should ever take non-Christians into partnership with them. As in every circumstance, however, I would advise you to follow the leading of the Lord concerning your situation.

The Bible says that though we are not *of* the world, we are still *in* it. So at some point, we have to deal with non-Christians in all walks of life. That is our opportunity to witness to these people.

I believe the best advice on how to deal with non-Christian businesses is for you to walk your life before these people by dealing with them honestly and fairly and by being up front with them on your expectations. Require that they fulfill their commitments as you would in any business dealing. Be firm and do not allow them to take advantage of you because you are a Christian. Such behavior gives Christians a reputation for being wimps, and we're not wimps—we're winners!

Q. What does the Word say about women working outside the home? Is she to trust God to provide through her husband?

A. The woman in Proverbs 31 is a working woman. Not only does she work outside the home, but she keeps her priorities straight—her home comes first and then her job. I believe if a woman chooses to work outside the home, she must keep her priorities straight—she must make sure that her husband, children, and, above all, her relationship with the Lord take precedence in her life. I know many women who are able to work and maintain their homes and minister to their husbands and children. It may be difficult, but it can be done.

Some women find themselves having to work due to financial necessity. If a woman does not have to work outside the home and she has young children, it is best for the children for her to stay home and take care of them. Work should not be used as an escape from parental responsibilities for the mother. In that case, the children will sense rejection and in later years may rebel. If a woman can trust the Lord to provide through her husband, then by all means she should.

Q. I teach earth science and biology in a public high school. I try to give equal weight to the views of evolution and creationism. Satan has tried to stop my witness by trying to get me fired. What rights do I have as a Christian and an American to witness in my school?

A. I praise the Lord for Christian teachers in our public schools! We do need you there, and I am praying for you! Even though we are not part of the world, we are still in the world (John 15:19; I John 4:17).

You are not to preach or force your doctrine upon your students. Even though you use certain textbooks that do not promote God's views, you can still present God's facts—but you do need to realize that your job in the public school might be in jeopardy.

You can minister to students on a one-on-one basis outside the classroom; but when it is time for class, you need to teach the assigned subject matter. If the administrator tells you that you cannot witness or minister on school grounds, then you cannot—although you can always do it off school property. Ask your administrator if you can start a Teens-for-Christ group and meet before or after school, whether it is at school or at an off-campus location.

There are special Christian groups that can help with further details. I would suggest you contact such a group in your area because state laws vary. Because there are so many legal ramifications, I am not qualified to answer your question regarding "legal" rights.

Q. Is it scriptural for a woman to be a pastor or a leader in the Church? I would particularly like you to address Paul's statements in I Corinthians 14:34-36.

A. The answer to your question regarding women in the ministry is found in I Timothy 2:11-15. If we are to interpret these verses literally, then we must go to the Greek for a clear understanding of their meaning.

When verse 11 says, *"Let the women learn in silence with all subjection,"* the emphasis is to be put on the word *silence.* Up to this time the women were not allowed to learn in a teaching setting. They were set apart in a separate place in the synagogue where they nursed their babies and exchanged the latest gossip while the men sat under teachers and received instruction. Here

Paul is actually exalting the place of women and telling them in modern vernacular, "be quiet and learn!"

Verse 12 says, *"But I suffer not a woman to teach, nor to usurp authority over the man, but to be in silence."* Paul is saying that although the women are now permitted to learn instructive teaching, they are not to take this new-found freedom and usurp authority over the men. The word "authority" in the Greek is the word *authenteo*, meaning "to act on one's OWN authority." So, this does not eliminate a woman teaching under her husband's authority and covering.

The word *silence* in the second part of the verse comes from a Greek word that actually means "tranquillity arising from within"—in other words, a quality of the spirit. Paul is saying, "Don't have a boisterous spirit when you teach; but remain under your husband's authority with a meek, tranquil, and quiet spirit."

In regard to women as leaders, we see several examples throughout the Old and New Testament where women held "leadership" positions. Some were prophetesses (Philip's four daughters in Acts 21:9), teachers (Priscilla in Acts 18:26), and servants/deacons (Phebe in Romans 16:1). Phebe was "*. . . a servant of the church which is at Cenchrea.*" The Greek word for *servant* is *diakonons*. When I looked it up in the Greek, I found that this word is the same one that we use for deacon. I also believe in I Timothy 3:11,12 that Paul's description of the requirement for a deacon's wife could be referring to women deacons as well.

To explain I Corinthians 14:34-36, we must look at the verse that precedes them. In verse 33 Paul is talking about not having confusion in the churches. The women sat in a separate part of the synagogue from the men. According to the custom of that day if a woman had questions concerning the sermon, the only man she could publicly address was her husband. Paul is telling the women in this verse not to call across the room to have their questions answered, because it caused confusion. He tells them to ask their questions at home. So this scripture is talking about husband and wife relationships, rather than a woman's relationship with the church.

Chapter Fourteen

SHARING YOUR FAITH

Q. Marilyn, can you give me some guidelines that will help me distinguish between a cult and the "real thing"?

A. One day the Pharisees were together and Jesus asked them a very significant question: ". . . *What think ye of Christ? whose son is he?* . . . " (Matthew 22:42). Jesus went on to prove through the Scriptures that the Christ was the Son of God and, therefore, He was God. Jesus said that Peter's revelation that Jesus was the Christ was given to him by the Father (Matthew 16:17).

You can use this same question to determine if a group is a cult or truly followers of Christ. If their answers confirm that Jesus Christ is the Son of God made flesh Who alone can redeem men from their sins, then you know it's the "real thing." Nevertheless, you must listen carefully to their entire message. Many cults use the same words and phrases that Christians use; however, they assign different meanings to those words. One well-known cult says that Jesus' blood atoned for original sin (Adam's fall), but you earn salvation from your own sins through good works and participation in the cult's ordinances and sacraments. The words are right but the doctrine is wrong.

A cult is a group which purports to lift up Jesus but denies some or all of the basic truths concerning His divine person, His virgin birth, and salvation through His blood. Many even deny the sinful nature of man. Cults nearly always add their own writings to the Bible, and they do not teach Christ's finished work at Calvary; salvation then becomes a system of "religious" human works. Evil spirits inspire the false doctrine of cults and blind the followers from the truth that Christ Jesus has come in the flesh.

Q. I have been studying with Jehovah's Witnesses. They say that the baptism mentioned in Ephesians 4:5 means that baptism as practiced by their group is the only true baptism. Do you agree?

A. Paul wrote in I Corinthians 12:13 that by one spirit we are all baptized into one body. Though there are many types of baptisms spoken of in Scripture, when Paul said there is one baptism (Ephesians 4:5), he was referring to the fact that the Holy Spirit—one Holy Spirit—baptized each one of us into the Body of Christ when we confessed the Lord Jesus as our Savior. It's a supernatural work done by the Holy Spirit when the person receives the Lord.

Jehovah's Witnesses do not believe that Jesus is God—they do not believe in His completed work of redemption at Calvary. I would warn you, therefore, to discontinue your studies with them because they are not teaching true salvation through the Lord Jesus Christ. Salvation isn't by way of a denomination, a cult, or man's ideas—it's by the shed blood of the Lord Jesus Christ.

Q. My husband was once born again and Spirit-filled. He became sexually involved with a cultist and has since joined that group. I have tried to show him this is wrong, but he gets mad at me. How should I witness to him?

A. First of all, bathe your husband with prayer and fasting; then read some good books on witnessing to this particular cult. Don't hammer at your husband, but show him your love and concern. Stand against Satan and command the spiritual blindness to leave your husband. Fight a spiritual warfare according to II Corinthians 10:3-5—you have authority over this situation, and you can win!

Q. Is the Seventh Day Adventist church a cult like the Mormons?

A. The Seventh Day Adventist church is not a cult. Their doctrine concerning salvation is correct—repentance of sin and acceptance of Jesus as Lord and Savior. They do believe in keeping the Old Testament Sabbath and are legalistic in some aspects. However, any group that teaches salvation through the shed blood of Jesus Christ and the finished work of Calvary is not a cult. Mormons, on the other hand, use terminology that is familiar to us but means something quite contrary to the Scriptures. For example, salvation to them is being baptized into and belonging to the Mormon church.

Q. I'm not sure I know how to lead someone to the Lord. Are there any specific "rules" I should follow? What do I say?

A. Any Christian can lead someone to the Lord, so let me first encourage you not to succumb to fear or worry about what to say. Pray first and ask the Lord to fill your mouth with the words He would have you say. Then, follow this simple scriptural approach:

1. Open a Bible to Romans 10. Have the candidate read aloud verses 9 and 10.
2. Explain to the candidate that because these scriptures say that "*. . . confession is made unto salvation,*" you are going to lead him in a short prayer. Ask the candidate to repeat after you as you pray.
3. Allow the Holy Spirit to guide your prayer so that the candidate will be sure to
   - Acknowledge that he is a sinner (repentance).
   - Ask the Father to cleanse him, by the blood of Jesus, from every sin he has committed—from the day he was born to this very moment.
   - Invite Jesus to come into his heart and to be Master and Lord of his life.
   - Thank God for saving his soul.
4. Ask the candidate to read Romans 10:13 aloud. Now, ask him to read it again, but this time have him substitute his own name for "whosoever" in this verse.

The candidate will realize that he has fulfilled the simple requirements of verse 13 and that he is saved according to God's Word, whether or not he feels any different!

You may warmly affirm this momentous decision and welcome your new brother or sister to the Body of Christ.

Q. What can I do to help a friend receive the baptism in the Holy Spirit?

A. The candidate for the baptism in the Holy Spirit must be a born-again child of God. The work of the Holy Spirit is essential for Christian growth. Through this baptism God empowers the believer to develop and express his new life in Jesus Christ.

Many people desire to be baptized in the Holy Spirit, but they don't know how to do so. Frequently, I open the conversation by saying, "I would love to pray with you to receive the baptism with the Holy Spirit." Then I proceed to

1. Open a Bible to Luke 11:10-13 and ask the candidate to read this passage aloud. These verses establish the way to receive the baptism in the Holy Spirit. We simply "ask" in faith because we know that our loving heavenly Father would never give us a "counterfeit."
2. Ask the candidate to read Acts 2:4 aloud. Assure the candidate that just as Jesus' disciples spoke in tongues when the Holy Spirit came upon them, the candidate will also speak in tongues when baptized in the Holy Spirit.
3. Ask the candidate to read Romans 8:26-28 aloud. This will confirm the purpose and the benefits of praying in "tongues."
4. Lead the candidate in a short prayer during which he asks the Father to baptize him with the Holy Spirit. Now tell the candidate that, by faith, you are going to pray in the Spirit *together*. Encourage the candidate to speak freely—as the Holy Spirit directs—regardless of how it may sound to the natural ear.

5. You, the leader, should begin to pray aloud in tongues.

After you have prayed together in tongues for awhile, you may wish to sing in the Spirit (I Corinthians 14:15).

Although the baptism in the Holy Spirit is a one-time event, the "infilling" of the Holy Spirit goes on and on and never stops. Encourage your friend to pray in the Spirit every day and to expect to find a new richness in his Christian experience.

Chapter Fifteen

LOVE • SEX • MARRIAGE • CHILDREN

Q. My husband was a Christian before we got married, but has since backslidden and gotten into drugs. Is it OK for me to get a separation until he decides to get off drugs and return to the Lord?

A. You need to hear from God about whether a separation is in order. Sometimes love must be tough, and there are times when God will direct us to bring about enough discomfort in another individual to cause them to seek help. I do not think that your situation is good or that you should just sit and wait for your husband to change. He's not going to change until he gets so uncomfortable that he has to begin to look at himself.

Although I cannot make this decision for you, the Lord will give you wisdom as you commune with Him. Begin feeding on His Word daily and praying on a consistent basis. As you seek Him first, the answer to your question will come. In the meantime, remember that Jesus has been made unto you wisdom and that you have the mind of Christ (see I Corinthians 1:30; 2:16). As you stand on these verses, God will reveal His perfect will for you.

Q. Why should the wife be submissive to the husband? Aren't they to be equal?

A. The reason the wife should submit to the husband is because God commands it (see Ephesians 5:22; Colossians 3:18). The word *submit* means "to be in marching order." Such order eliminates confusion and strife not only in a home, but in every area of life.

Can you imagine what a company would be like if there was no head of the company or no one to make a final decision? Even within the Trinity, the Father, Son, and Holy Spirit are equal . . . but the latter two are submitted to God the Father. God's wisdom dictates that there must be order in every relationship.

Submission does not mean inequality, it simply establishes a priority of order for the sake of harmony. This does not mean that a wife has no input into a decision which is made—I certainly help in the decision making in my household—but whenever there is a conflict, my husband always will make the final decision. It is rare, however, that we disagree on a decision; so there is continual harmony in our home because our home is established on God's order of headship.

Q. Does the Lord give direction to the wife through the husband, even if he is not serving God? This is a matter dealing with my career.

A. Though I think this should really be a matter of prayer, there is no doubt that a husband might give godly direction to a wife, even though he isn't serving the Lord. If a Christian wife is praying for her husband and believing for him to be the proper head of their home, an unsaved husband certainly can give wise direction. A wife can receive answers from her unsaved husband, depending upon the attitude of her heart. A husband can confirm a wife's decision if she is lovingly submitted to him and if his opinions about her career are valid and in line with what the Holy Spirit is telling her.

Q. What does the Bible say about birth control? As Christians, should we or should we not use contraceptives?

A. The greatest gift the Lord has given us besides Himself is our free will—the right of free choice. We are privileged to commit ourselves to Him and to seek His guidance in all of our decisions. This also applies to the number of children a couple may decide to have. Although children are a blessed inheritance from the Lord (see Psalms 127:3), I do not believe that God created us for the purpose of bringing children into the world, but for the purpose of fellowship and union with Himself.

Birth control became an issue in the church because of a misinterpretation of Genesis 38:9. Onan refused to "raise up" children in his dead brother's name. Onan's sin was not refusing to father children, but refusing to father children who would carry his brother's name. Verse 10 says this rebellion so displeased God that He slew Onan.

The decision to use birth control is between you and God. Under no circumstances, however, should abortion be considered an acceptable form of birth control.

Q. Is it a sin if a married woman whose husband is unable to produce seed is artificially inseminated?

A. The matter of artificial insemination is not mentioned, of course, in the Bible. However, I have many reservations against any woman conceiving through the seed of an unknown man. There are the obvious possibilities of unknown spiritual and physical generational curses, and there may be legal problems in years to come as well. There are better options for Christian couples than that of utilizing the seed of an unknown man—pray to be able to conceive children or to qualify for adoption (Mark 11:24).

Q. A woman recently expressed her love for my husband. Together we met with her because we thought this was the correct and loving way to handle the situation. She is persisting in her pursuit of him. What should we do?

A. I can't tell you the number of women who have experienced the problem you've described. You are blessed to have a husband who is faithful. Be certain that you continue to walk in love toward this woman, but do not let her cause strife between you and your husband.

Let your husband know that you appreciate him. Be consistent in affirming his trust and faithfulness; and spend a great deal of time praying in the Spirit, binding the spirit of lust in this woman (Ephesians 6:18). Also, I would not view this lady as a threat, but rather as a person in need of much prayer, love, and forgiveness.

I would suggest that you and your husband discuss this problem with your pastor. If the woman is a Christian and repents of her behavior, she is to be forgiven; but if she doesn't repent, the Scripture tells us she is to be excommunicated from the church (Matthew 18:15-17). If the woman isn't a Christian but a coworker or employee, I would make any contact with her as brief and as distant as possible.

Q. You said that a husband has a right to leave/divorce his wife if she does not go to bed with him. What about if the husband is an alcoholic, a womanizer, or the like? One woman decided to be a good Christian wife and have sex with her husband, and now she has AIDS. Another woman I know contracted herpes from her husband.

A. Thank you for allowing me to comment on the sexual relationship in marriage. Women are told to submit to their own husbands as unto the Lord, but nowhere in the Bible are they told to submit to the devil or to demon spirits (I Corinthians 3:16,17). I do not think that "submission" in the sexual relationship includes having to submit to a partner who has a venereal disease such as herpes or AIDS or who is physically out of control due to drug or alcohol consumption. I would add that every believer needs to follow the leading of the Holy Spirit regarding the situation in which you find yourself (Colossians 3:15,16; Hebrews 4:12).

Q. My boyfriend and I have been dating for 2½ years. We split up two months after we were engaged because he got cold feet and didn't want to be faithful to me for the rest of our lives. He is not a Christian, and I wonder if we were supposed to split up. Please help me understand this.

A. The Bible admonishes believers not to be unequally yoked together with unbelievers (see II Corinthians 6:14). I am very certain that it is not God's will for you to marry an unbeliever. He has a godly mate just for you who will help you grow in your Christian walk. I would pray for God to save your exfiance, but I would not pray for his return into your life. Ask God to speak to you concerning this area of your life; and as He speaks, obey.

Q. Are there any "ten commandments" for newlyweds for a successful marriage? Especially for one who is a new Christian but married to an unbeliever?

A. There are no "ten commandments" as such for newlyweds for a successful marriage, but there are several scriptures which would apply. They are listed as follows: Proverbs 31; I Corinthians 7:3,4,14; 13:1-13; Ephesians 5:21-25; and the book of I John. One of my favorite scriptures to give to newlyweds is *"Do nothing from selfishness or empty conceit, but with humility of mind let each of you regard one another as more important than himself"* (Philippians 2:3 NAS). The entire chapter of Philippians 2 is a good example of the mind and attitude that husbands and wives need to have toward each other. This is set out as an example for the entire Body of Christ, and it is certainly applicable in marriage.

Q. My husband is a wonderful husband, father, provider, and is a godly man; but he is not a social person. He desires fellowship with very few people. How do I explain this to brothers and sisters in the Lord? I hate making excuses for him.

A. With so many attributes to his credit, I'm sure it must be difficult to understand and explain to others that your husband is not a very sociable person. I'd suggest that you not try to explain him to others. When others approach you with an invitation, simply tell them that your husband is the head of your house and request that they ask him for a response. This will place the burden of the acceptance or refusal upon his shoulders and relieve you from making any excuses at all.

Q. Is there such a thing as sexual perversion between husband and wife?

A. Hebrews 13:4 says the marriage bed is undefiled. *Undefiled* in the Greek indicates there will be no "tainting" nor perverted sexual behavior. I believe oral sex, anal sex, and the like have to do with perverted behavior. Many Christians have argued with me about this, but I stand fast. We certainly agree that oral and anal sex is wrong between males—why would it be right between a male and female? These forms of sexual intercourse are certainly unnatural, because they misuse the body and pervert the natural function for which God created it (Romans 1:26).

Q. Is it wrong for Christian couples to watch movies that may have nudity in them? I'm not referring to X-rated pornography—I'm talking about cable movies which have some nudity.

A. Movies with any type of nudity, whether soft pornography or hard core, are wrong. There are many references throughout the Bible that say looking upon the nakedness of another is sin (see Leviticus 18; Revelation 3:17,18). To indulge in viewing this type of nudity is an open door for Satan because it feeds the fleshly appetites and eventually will lead to the desire for more.

You are giving demons of lust permission to enter your home through your television. You need to put a stop to this immediately! Ask the Lord to forgive you and your husband, and then cleanse your home and close any open doors Satan might have entered because of your television viewing.

Q. Marilyn, why is there so much incest in the Bible?

A. According to Paul the things recorded in the Old Testament such as incest were given for "*. . . our examples to the intent we should not lust after evil things, as they also lusted*" (I Corinthians 10:6). It goes on to tell us not to do the things that they did since we would also incur the same curse or judgment that they experienced. Second Timothy 3:16 tells us that all scripture is given for instruction, reproof, and training. The Bible gives us a record of how God responds to sin and how He rewards righteousness.

Q. My family background is very weak in the area of sexual purity. I was sexually molested as a child. How can I plant "good seeds" in my children's lives so that they will remain sexually pure as they grow up?

A. Even though Christians are under grace, we still suffer from sickness, disease, death, and even generation bondages; so we still have to appropriate the freedom Christ gave us in Galatians 3:13. We have to drive off the "giants" of generational bondages, just like the Hebrew children had to drive the giants out of the land that God gave to them. The good news is we can be free from these curses through Jesus' redemptive blood. Command the curse to be broken in the name of Jesus, and speak the covering of the blood of Jesus over your family. The blood will cleanse your family from all unrighteousness.

I also encourage you to be very honest with your children

concerning your background. Tell them how Satan comes into families and passes curses from generation to generation. Give them the same Biblical steps that you have used to cast down strongholds in your life. Also Harrison House has published an excellent book titled, PRAYERS THAT AVAIL MUCH. This book contains prayers that are powerful in protecting and keeping your children free.

Q. Is lust and sexual perversion considered to be demon possession?

A. Lust and sexual perversion are works of the flesh, but that does not mean that Satan does not influence these fleshly desires (see Galatians 5:19). People with lust and sexual perversion are not necessarily demon possessed, but they can be. It is also possible for people to be possessed with a spirit of lust and sexual perversion if they are not Christians. If a Christian is participating in this type of activity, then it is a work of the flesh which may have opened the door to demonic oppression.

Q. My daughter was abused sexually by her father. What should I do?

A. God charges Christian parents to care for their children, so you must take action. First report your daughter's father to the proper authorities. The law requires that cases like this be reported, and you will be breaking the law if you do not report him.

If you have done all these things, then confront this man directly. Ask him to go for counseling. He was probably abused as a child himself, and he needs to be set free from this bondage.

It is important for your daughter to understand that God loves her very much; and that she is not a bad person. Let her know that what her father did is not her fault; it is something that the devil encouraged him to do, and it was wrong.

Don't allow the devil to get a stronghold in your daughter's mind. I suggest you help her find Nehemiah 8:10, and have her daily meditate and say out loud that *"The joy of the Lord is my strength."* And as she meditates this scripture, tell her to also meditate on how much Jesus loves her.

You cannot simply pass over this transgression and pretend that it doesn't exist. This sin has brought a curse upon your house. I would not give Satan any room in this area—it needs to be dealt with immediately.

Q. I have found out that my husband is a bisexual and a pedophile. I am praying for God to save his soul, but I am also thinking of getting a divorce. We have four children, and I'm not sure what to do.

A. I was grieved to hear of your husband's sexual sin. Matthew 19:9 tells us that although God hates divorce, He allows it when fornication is involved. Fornication has to do with more than adultery: it includes any sexual deviance.

Several things must be taken into consideration with a divorce of this nature: (1) Is your husband willing to repent of this sinful lifestyle and return to you? (2) Will he pursue this deviant behavior with your children? If so, then you must remove yourself from that situation. If he is fondling little children, then this is a clear indication that the welfare of your children may be at stake.

Your husband is in a very serious situation which requires a great deal of prayer and fasting. This evil can be broken in his life, but he must first be willing. I would also advise you to find a Spirit-filled Christian counselor and to ask your husband to submit to counseling. If he is not willing to take any steps of action toward repentance and reconciliation, then a separation may be in order while you pray for God to change him.

Through the power of the Holy Spirit, you can remain free from bitterness. Forgive your husband on a daily basis so that bitterness will not defile you and cause you harm (Hebrews 12:15).

Q. I am 15 years old and I am struggling with pressure from my friends. I've always wanted to please other people so they would like me, but how do I draw the line?

A. We must not be so concerned about what others think that we can't follow the instructions of the Lord (see Proverbs 29:25). Successful people follow God's opinion—not man's. Also, Philippians 2:4 says, *"Look not every man on his own things, but every man also on the things of others."* In this scripture, Paul presents the balance between serving God and serving man: we are to become like Jesus and serve one another. Keep your eyes on the Lord, and it will be easier not to give in to peer pressure.

Q. I have a six-month-old daughter and a two-year-old son who are precious gifts from the Lord. I want so much to raise them to know the Lord, but my mother-in-law is fearful that we may "overdo the religious training" and cause them to turn away from the Lord. Is this possible?

A. We can never spoil or "overtrain" our children by giving them too much love or too much Bible! I suggest that parents read God's Word to their children and play scripture tapes for them. Throughout the day sing scripture songs and choruses so the children can hear them. The Bible promises that the Word of God will never return void, so parents can be assured that the good seeds they plant in their children now will bear fruit in later life.

The two elements for effectively training your children are love and discipline. In dealing with your children, you need 100 percent of both these elements. You cannot train a child whom you don't love; and you cannot love a child whom you don't train.

Love and discipline go hand in hand. Trust the Holy Spirit to teach you how to train each individual child in every phase of life. God is faithful to help parents in this way.

Q. As Christians, how important is it to send our children to a Christian school?

A. I believe in this age of humanistic education that it is very important for a child to attend Christian school or have a home school. Home schooling is an excellent alternative to a Christian school, provided that you comply with the laws of your state and use a good, sound curriculum. You must take into consideration that home schooling is a full-time job; and in order for the program to be successful, you must be consistent and dedicated in the training and disciplining of your children. I would encourage any parent, who is able to home school their children and cannot afford a Christian school, to do so.

Christian education in general is simply an education based upon the Biblical principles of God's Word. This differs from the public schools, which base their education upon humanistic philosophy—a philosophy which says that "each man determines what is right in his or her own eyes," and that we can "be as gods." A Christian education teaches a student that Jesus is the supreme Head of the Church, and God is a supreme, supernatural being Who exists, is loving and caring, and sent Jesus as His only Son to die for us.

However, there are many concerned Christian parents who are financially unable to send their children to a Christian school. In this case, the parents should pray for their children, their teachers, and the schools. God is able to supply Christian teachers in a public school environment. Parents should also become watchdogs over what the children are taught, discuss with the children what they are learning, and voice disapproval to teachers, administrators, and school boards about humanistic, godless material.

Q. I stay at home with my two children. I have all the patience in the world with my two-year-old boy, but I have bad feelings toward my four-year-old. I spank him and yell at him when I'm angry and just don't seem to have any control. What is causing me to be hostile with my own child?

A. I would encourage you to get in touch with a Spirit-filled charismatic church in your area and talk with the pastor there. It seems that you have some bitterness and unforgiveness toward someone in your past. Although you may have suppressed this anger or resentment, it is coming out in your relationship with your children. Be assured that you are not a hateful person, but something in your past is manifesting itself and needs to be dealt with immediately. I encourage you to see a Christian counselor in spite of the cost. It will be well worth it to your children's future to work through this problem and be healed from your past.

Q. My husband has left me for the ninth time. Everything seems to be closing in on me. We have a 4½ month-old baby who cries for hours on end. I get so nervous, I spank him. I'm afraid I'm becoming an abusive parent. I love my husband, but I don't think I can live like this. What's wrong with me?

A. A baby as young as yours is too young to spank. Your baby is crying because of the fear, strife, and anger that is coming from you and your husband. You need counseling right away, and you need to overcome any pride that would keep you from counseling with your pastor or a Spirit-filled counselor. You should consider leaving your baby with family members or trustworthy friends for a few hours a day or for a period of time. This will help you to have some time alone to seek God and to sort out your thoughts. You have a serious situation that should not be ignored.

Q. Can we ever use as a punishment or discipline the

memorization of God's Word? Would this do more harm than good? Also, I have four lovely daughters, but one of them is so different from the others. She can be so wonderful, but then turn around and be absolutely stubborn and rebellious. Is it possible that she is demon-possessed?

A. I do not believe it is ever a good idea to punish your children by having them memorize God's Word—I see nowhere in the Scriptures where we should do this. I believe that it would make God's Word appear to be something distasteful to your children, rather than something that is a delight to read and enjoy, and thereby grow.

Also, I believe that the only time loving parents should spank is when they are calm—not angry. Every time your children are spanked, they should be held, loved, and assured by the Word of God that you discipline them because you love them (Proverbs 13:24). Children must never be beaten—this is abuse, and I do not condone it.

I doubt that your daughter is oppressed by a demon. Different children have different personalities, and God uses these personalities as strengths in His overall plan for each child's life. However, you do need to deal with the stubbornness and rebellion with firm but loving discipline. Take spiritual authority over her life, and tell the devil you will not allow him any room for spirits to operate in her.

Q. What do you think about Santa Claus, the Tooth Fairy, and the Easter Bunny? Should Christian parents tell their children about them?

A. The scripture warns us not to give heed to "fables" (see I Timothy 1:4). The Greek word for fables is "*muthos*," which means "anything delivered by word of mouth," such as legendary tales like the Easter Bunny, Tooth Fairy, or Santa Claus. A fable is a "foolish or improbable story" (II Timothy 4:4; Titus 1:14;

II Peter 1:16). I believe very strongly that parents should always speak the truth; and Santa Claus, the Tooth Fairy, and the Easter Bunny are not the truth.

Q. Could you give me your opinion on celebrating holidays such as Valentine's Day, birthdays, anniversaries, Mother's and Father's Day, and Grandparent's Day?

A. God loves holidays and celebrations, and He established many of them in the Old Testament. Holidays like the ones you mentioned are fine if they are kept in reference to celebrating the work of God in our lives. God has never been against us having fun—He has only been against us putting the fun ahead of Him (I Corinthians 10:31).

Q. Are alternative celebrations on Halloween OK for Christians?

A. Halloween originally started as the eve of All Saints' Day. The early church celebrated All Saints' Day in commemoration of the martyred saints of the early church. The word *Halloween* is derived from ''all hallowed (holy) eve,'' or in other words, the eve of All Saints' Day. Halloween started out as a wonderful holiday, and then Satan distorted it.

I don't believe there is anything wrong with having alternatives to Halloween, as long as they are godly and do not exalt witches, demons, etc. Anything that exalts Satan is wrong and should be avoided. I don't believe there is anything wrong with having a costume party or other such things as long as the costumes do not portray those things involved with the occult. Anytime we dabble with the occult, we are asking for big trouble; and I strongly warn you against such activities.

Q. I have a son who ''feels'' bound by homosexuality. He is only 17 and lives at home. He has no lovers, but has been called ''gay'' and a "fag" by kids since kindergarten. How can I help him?

A. I feel impressed to tell you that one's self-image is developed by hearing what others believe about us. Because your son has heard this satanic lie for so long, these words have acted like seeds and have taken root in his spirit, creating a very negative self-image. This self-image can be broken by believing more strongly who God says he is. You must also see your son as God sees him.

Stop confessing that he is bound by homosexuality—he has never committed this sinful act, so he is not a homosexual! Begin getting a vision of God for your son; and talk the vision, not your fears. God created the worlds with His spoken words, and we can create our children's world by the negative or positive words we speak to them.

I believe you need to reveal this information to your son and begin having him confess God's image about himself. I also recommend that you find a Spirit-filled Christian counselor—preferably a man—who can move in the gifts of the Spirit and help your son get free from this poor image. I am praying that he will be set totally free and that Satan can no longer harass him in this area.

Q. I have young children and I do not feel comfortable with the cartoon programs on television. How can I know which ones are acceptable for them to watch?

A. Anything which interferes with your relationship with the Lord is wrong—including cartoons. Jesus warned us to be careful what we see and hear because this can affect our spiritual lives—what we sow into our hearts, we will reap from our hearts (Proverbs 23:7; Mark 4:24). Cartoons can feed negative, ungodly things to our spirits—and these will affect us later. Be very cautious never to let your children watch cartoons which have occultic or demonic implications. Anything that uses demons, violence, and humanistic philosophy should be avoided. Children subconsciously pick up such philosophies very quickly, and I would not allow them to watch anything on television which promotes that type of thinking.

Chapter Sixteen

DIVORCE • REMARRIAGE FAMILY PROBLEMS

Q. My second husband committed adultery and physically abused me. If he becomes born again, should I remarry him or am I to spend the rest of my life without a husband?

A. It is perfectly acceptable if you desire a reconciliation with your ex-husband. If, however, he has remarried, then you need to pray and release this situation to the Lord. If he has not remarried, you can claim Mark 10:8,9 and Colossians 1:20,21.

I also recommend that you begin praying I Corinthians 1:30; 2:16. As you stand on these verses, God will reveal His perfect will for you. Should you decide to remarry your ex-husband, I would recommend that both of you seek counseling with a Spirit-filled Christian counselor in your area.

Q. My husband and I are divorced but we are still having sex on weekends. I am feeling that this isn't quite right. What do you think?

A. I do not believe that sex between divorced couples is ever right. Once a couple is divorced, they are no longer married in the eyes of the state, and the only time the Bible permits sex is in a marriage relationship (Hebrews 13:4).

Q. Can a born-again Christian remarry if they were divorced before becoming a Christian?

A. If a person has divorced and subsequently becomes born again, then I believe the person is free to remarry because all past sins have been forgiven, including divorce. Not only do old things pass away at the moment of new birth, but new Christians are given a totally new beginning (II Corinthians 5:17,21). Any marriage that has been dissolved prior to one's salvation was not under covenant relationship and, therefore, not in fellowship with Jesus Christ.

Q. If two believers have been married before God, then the Bible says a valid marriage has taken place. If neither spouse commits adultery, then isn't that marriage indissoluble? If either party remarries under the above circumstances, does not he or she commit adultery?

A. If married partners in a second marriage have genuinely repented of their sin of divorce and all that led to the divorce, then they are totally forgiven. That first marriage is under the blood of Jesus and in God's eyes is forgiven. When God forgives, He forgets all sin (see Psalms 103:12).

Q. I have a divorced friend who is in our singles group. Is she a widow in God's eyes? Is God her husband and the father of her children, spiritually speaking? I have not been able to find the answer to this. Can you help me?

A. The word *widow* comes from the Hebrew root word which means "forsaken," so this includes divorcees as well as widows. God supports, defends, and vindicates all single parents and assumes the responsibility as a parent to their children (see Psalms 146:9). In those hours when loneliness and responsibility seem to overwhelm the single person, Psalms 146:9 can be meditated upon because it will bring great comfort and help.

Q. Marilyn, my husband and I are separated because he is in terrible bondage to every lust of the flesh, even to the point of mental illness. Is it Biblical for me to keep my three-year-old son from his father and to refuse reconciliation until he seeks deliverance and is walking with God? Terrible oppression fills our home after my husband visits.

A. It is very scriptural for you to protect your son and make a Christian stand before the Lord. If you can legally protect your child from the damaging effects his father has upon him, then you should do so; however, it is important for you also to comply with the law and any visitation rights the courts have given to your husband. There is definitely a spiritual danger to your son if he is around spirits of lust and depression. For the legal aspects of this situation, I suggest you seek your lawyer's advice.

Q. I would like to know if I Corinthians 7:15 means that a woman can remarry if she pleases?

A. First Corinthians 7:12-16 is speaking of an unequally yoked relationship where one of the mates has come to Christ sometime after the marriage ceremony. God, in His mercy, has made provision for this situation so that the entire household may be under His covering. In this type of relationship, the believer is free to marry if the unbelieving mate decides to terminate the relationship of his or her own free will. However, if the unbelieving mate chooses to remain, then both the unbelieving mate and any children of this union are sanctified by the believer; and God is free to bless this family according to the pleasure of His will.

Q. How are we to know what generation curses to break for our adopted daughter?

A. Each child has a different background so I really don't know what curses need to be broken in your adopted child's life. I have an adopted son, so I have watched for traits that I felt indicated a generation curse—patterns of behavior that definitely did not follow the standards that he had been taught in our home. Some of the things I have come against include rebellion, immorality, lying, insecurities, fears, anxieties, and failure.

Watch for those noticeable things that are of a real negative nature. Then minister to your daughter so she can stand against them too. If there is any possible way you can learn about her family, you would know more specifically how to pray. We had the opportunity to meet my son's natural father and saw some of the same patterns in him that my son was manifesting; as a result, we knew what generation curses to break.

Q. I think my old weaknesses before Jesus became Lord of my life stem from my birth mother. I was adopted as a baby and met my birth mother three years ago. In seeing her, I could see some of my own weaknesses.

A. The weaknesses in your own nature can very possibly stem from your birth mother. These would be ''handed down to you'' in the form of a generational curse. You can break every family curse through Jesus' redemptive blood. Command the curse to be broken in the name of Jesus, and claim the cleansing that His blood has provided for you. Some additional scriptures concerning this include Deuteronomy 27,28; Psalms 68:6; and Proverbs 12:7; 24:3.

Q. My aging parents seem to have become my responsibility since I live close to them. I am thankful to have them still living, but they often won't listen to my opinions—they just do as they please. As they get older, will I have to take the role of a parent?

A. We are told to honor our father and mother (Deuteronomy 5:16). The word *honor* means, ''to be heavy or weighty, to promote, to glorify.'' Grown children have a responsibility to make sure that their parents are well cared for, but I do not believe we should interfere in their lives.

If your parents become senile, then your situation will change. However, as long as they are able to care for themselves, do not take on the heavy responsibility of making decisions for them, as much as you might disagree with their choices. If you treat them like children, they will act more and more childish because your own spirit will begin to reflect this to them and reproduce it within them. Continue loving them as you have in the past; but beyond this, I encourage you simply to pray and intercede on their behalf. Trust the Lord to give them the wisdom they need to make their own decisions.

Q. My problem is my mother's attitude. She lives with us and is a very bitter person. My children are picking up the bad things she says. She complains about living with us and recently said that she wants to quit her job. What can I do about this?

A. I can see why you are troubled over the situation with your mother. After you have prayed, asked God for guidance, and submitted this matter to Him, you need to sit down and have a very honest conversation your mother. Explain to her the problem that she is creating; tell her that your home is your first priority, and she will have to cooperate with the family. If she is not happy with you, then she must find the means to get her own place.

Q. Should we invite my homosexual brother to our home for family gatherings? His "companion" is always with him. My brother is crazy about children—especially mine since they are his only niece and nephew, but I am concerned because of his lifestyle. What would you advise?

A. You need to have a very frank and firm talk with your brother. Tell him that you love him very much, but you are absolutely opposed to his homosexual lifestyle. If you can, give him scriptures to support what you are saying. You need to make it very plain that his consorts are not welcome and that you will not tolerate any attempts to present his lifestyle in a positive manner to your children.

You must also have a very open discussion about your brother with your children. This conversation, of course, will depend on their ages. Explain to them that homosexuality is against the Bible and that you believe the time will come when your brother will be saved and come out of that lifestyle. They are to love him right now, but not to go along with his ways. If your brother wants to be part of your family get-togethers with these ground rules, then make him welcome.

Chapter Seventeen

DEATH • DYING • GRIEF

Q. How should we explain the death of a child to Christian parents? I've heard people say the death happened because the child's angels were asleep or that the parents' faith wasn't strong enough.

A. Only God fully knows what has happened when tragedy strikes, and the death of a child is certainly a tragedy. When offering comfort in such a situation, be honest and say you don't know why this happened. Be available to listen, to pray with and for the family, to run errands, to prepare food, and to do anything else that needs to be done. And remember, many friends and family members will be ready to help for a few weeks. The parents may need you more after all the commotion subsides.

Matthew 18:10 speaks of angels who are assigned to children. I believe that this word "children" includes the children of God of any age. We know from Hebrews 1:14 that the angels are to minister for all of us who inherit salvation. Angels act on our behalf as we speak the Word of God and apply it to our lives. There is absolutely nothing in the Scriptures to indicate that the death of a child is because the angels have failed in their tasks.

God will always move according to His Word, and all His promises are sure to those who believe and claim them. If we are not operating the Word to change our circumstances, God must allow the circumstances. Nevertheless, we should never judge the the quality or quantity of the faith of another.

Q. Who causes death—God or the devil?

A. I'm so glad you asked this question. The Bible is very clear about this matter: "*The thief cometh not, but for to steal, and to kill, and to destroy: I am come that they might have life, and that they might have it more abundantly*" (John 10:10). Satan is the one who kills—Jesus gives life and gives it more abundantly.

First Corinthians 15:26 declares death to be an *enemy* of God. Nevertheless, the Bible promises that for those who love God *all* things will work together for their good; and I believe that includes the death of a loved one (Romans 8:28).

Q. How can I handle grief? I feel almost overwhelmed sometimes.

A. Unfortunately, there are difficult times for all of us when our loved ones die. I faced a similar situation when my own father died. One of my family members, however, was almost suffocating in grief. Her sorrow was so deep that I was concerned about her physical health. I prayed about her, and the Holy Spirit gave me the key to unlock this loved one's sorrow. He showed me that Jesus carried our sins, sicknesses, and griefs (Isaiah 53:3-5). Then I saw that this relative was not allowing Jesus to carry her grief; she was carrying it alone.

Now let me ask you, "Have you cast your burden of grief on the Lord?" Grief can give you a nervous breakdown. It can physically harm you, because you were not designed to carry it. Right now, cast your sorrows on Jesus. He said, "*Come unto me, all ye that labour and are heavy laden, and I will give you rest*" (Matthew 11:28).

Let Jesus carry your grief and bring the rest and refreshing of the Holy Spirit to your soul. You will find that the joy of the Lord is truly your strength.

Q. Where are the dead? I've heard that they are in heaven and I've also heard that they are sleeping in their graves.

A. The teaching that the dead are sleeping and know nothing is based on an Old Testament scripture: "*So man lieth down, and riseth not: till the heavens be no more, they shall not awake, nor be raised out of their sleep*" (Job 14:12). However, Jesus indicated that the dead do have consciousness when He told the parable about Lazarus and the rich man (Luke 16:20-31).

The New Testament also tells us that something exciting happened after Jesus' resurrection: *"By which also he [Christ] went and preached unto the spirits in prison"* (I Peter 3:19). Paul sheds more light on this topic: *" . . . when he [Christ] ascended on high, he led captivity captive, . . . "* (Ephesians 4:8). These scriptures tell us that Jesus preached to those who were imprisoned in death before Jesus' resurrection, and that Jesus "took captive" these people and took them with Him when He was resurrected from the dead.

The Scriptures are very clear on what happens when a Christian dies: *"We are confident, I say, and willing rather to be absent from the body, and to be present with the Lord:"* (II Corinthians 5:8). (Also see Philippians 1:21-24.) At the point of physical death the Christian is immediately in the Lord's presence.

The confusion about "sleep" comes from I Thessalonians 4:13. In this passage, the Greek word for "asleep" comes from the root word *keimai* which means "to lie down." This is talking about the dead physical body which is "laid" in the grave as in a sleep, while our spirits are with the Lord.

Q. Marilyn, please help us. What hope can we offer to our brother who is dying of AIDS?

A. First of all I want to encourage you to tell your brother of the saving love and grace of Jesus Christ—lead him in a prayer of salvation. That is the most important step.

In regard to healing, I believe it is always God's will to heal—even victims of AIDS. However, unless there is repentance of any behavior (immorality, drug abuse, and the like) which may have opened your brother to this disease, then healing will not solve the problem. God wants your brother to be truly free of every bondage, not just one disease. Encourage your brother to begin reading the Bible on a daily basis. Together, you can claim the promises of healing and abundant life that God says are the heritage of the righteous.

If your brother is not part of a solid, Bible-believing church, then help him find one that will stand with him through this illness. If he is too ill to attend church, then find a church that will bring ministry to him. I believe that Colossians 1:11 will be a wonderful prayer for your family. Be sure to personalize it like this, "We are strengthened with all might, according to Christ's glorious power, and we have His joyful patience and endurance."

Q. Is there ever a good excuse for a Christian to commit suicide?

A. There is *never* a reason for a Christian to commit suicide. Such an action contradicts everything the Scriptures promise and everything Jesus accomplished on the Cross for us: *"Nay, in all these things we are more than conquerors through him that loved us"* (Romans 8:37); and *"The eyes of your understanding being enlightened; that ye may know what is the hope of his calling, and what the riches of the glory of his inheritance in the saints, and what is the exceeding greatness of his power to us-ward who believe, according to the working of his mighty power"* (Ephesians 1:18-19).

Those Christians who have committed suicide have been deceived by the devil, who has convinced them that their situation is absolutely hopeless. Nevertheless, suicide is not an unforgivable sin. The suicide victim has not lost his/her salvation. My heart always aches for the family members who must deal with such a loss. There are several scriptures that I have found helpful at such a time: Psalms 25:16,17,20; 46:1; Isaiah 53:4; II Corinthians 2:14; and Philippians 4:7.

Anyone who is struggling with depression needs to find a Spirit-filled Christian counselor who will offer support and encouragement. This spirit of depression can be broken as a believer learns to look to God and His answers and not the circumstances.

Chapter Eighteen

PROPHECY AND THE END TIMES

Q. Where are we now in relation to the Bible's prophetic timetable?

A. Daniel 9:25-27 is one of the best prophetic "timetables" we have. Each week in the prophecy equals seven years for a total of 490 years. Sixty-nine weeks, or 483 years, were to transpire from the decree to rebuild Jerusalem until the Messiah appeared—an event which is historically verifiable. The last "week" or seven-year period is the Tribulation. We are presently in between the 69th and 70th week of this prophecy, a "break" in which God is dealing primarily with the Gentiles before resuming His plan for the Jews.

No one but God knows when Daniel's 70th week will begin; however, we are told to "occupy" until the Lord returns (Luke 19:13). This word *occupy* means "to trade in business"; therefore, we are to be about our Father's business until Jesus returns.

Q. When will the Tribulation take place?

A. There is much discussion among believers today as to whether the Tribulation will take place before or after the Rapture of the Church. I believe that it is very important that we not let the devil divide us on this subject. It is interesting to discuss and study the scriptures about end-time events; however, it is absolutely vital that we not forget Christ's commandment to love one another.

Christians are to be ready for the moment when Jesus comes back for us. Our lives and hearts are to line up with God's Word, and we must walk in holiness and love toward one another. Only God knows the exact timing of Christ's Second Coming.

Q. What is the Rapture? I can't find the word in my Bible.

A. The word "rapture" is not in the Bible. However, I Thessalonians 4:13-18 does clearly state in the Greek that believers will be "caught up" to be with Christ. Whatever you call it, the Scriptures teach it.

There is much discussion about the Rapture and when it will occur. People who believe in a pre-Tribulation rapture base this belief on references from II Thessalonians 2:6,7 (NAS): *"And you know what restrains him [the Antichrist] now, so that in his time he may be revealed . . . only he who now restrains will do so until he is taken out of the way."* This view states that the one restraining the Antichrist at this time is the Church. Revelation 3:10 and the parable of the bridegroom are also cited as proof of a "pre-trib" rapture.

Revelation 14:14-16 seems to indicate a rapture at the midpoint of the Tribulation. Those who believe in a post-Tribulation rapture, one occurring at the end of the Tribulation, base their stand on Matthew 24:13-31.

Quite frankly, your salvation does not depend on what you believe about the Rapture. It does depend on what you believe about Jesus Christ. There are many fascinating books on end-time events, but be sure as you read and study that you do not lose sight of the eternal life which is yours through believing in Jesus as your personal Savior.

Although I personally believe the Rapture will be pre-Tribulation, I refuse to argue or have any contention or strife over this subject. I believe the Body of Christ has been called into unity, and it is important to know that we all agree that Jesus is coming!

Q. Marilyn, I heard you say that the book of Revelation mentions three separate raptures. Where does it say that?

A. I believe that there are at least three raptures spoken of in the book of Revelation. The overcoming saints are raptured at the beginning of the great Tribulation (Revelation 4:1). In Revelation 11 we read of the rapture of the two witnesses. There is also a ''harvest rapture'' of Christians at the midpoint of the Tribulation (Revelation 14:14-16).

Q. What will happen to backslidden Christians during the Rapture?

A. Backslidden Christians will be left behind during the Rapture. Those taken up in the Rapture will be those *overcoming* Christians who have stayed in faith and in the Word (Revelation 2:26,27; 3:10). However, those who are backslidden and repent after the Rapture will become a part of the remnant Church. Also included in the remnant Church will be those people saved after the Rapture of the overcomers, and this includes the 144,000 Jews who will come in during this terrible time of Tribulation.

How do we become overcomers? We become overcomers by faith: *''For whatsoever is born of God overcometh the world: and this is the victory that overcometh the world, even our faith''* (I John 5:4). It is important for us during these end times to become very close to God and to distance ourselves from the world. Those people who become close to the world and lukewarm to God are placing themselves in a spiritually dangerous position. We can all be overcomers because Jesus has made us more than conquerors!

Q. Would you please tell me if the Holy Spirit will be on this earth after the Church is taken away?

A. The Holy Spirit will definitely be here during the Tribulation. The book of Revelation indicates that people will be saved during that time, which is not possible without the Holy Spirit. Jesus told us in the book of John that the Holy Spirit convicts the world of sin, righteousness, and judgment; that no man can come to the Father except by Jesus; and that the Holy Spirit is the One Who draws people to the Lord. (See John 15:26-16:16).

Q. Could you explain to me what the coming revival is all about?

A. The word "revival" means a lot of different things to different people, depending on your denominational background and upbringing. Perhaps you are referring to the outpouring that has been prophesied in the latest renewal that God has brought upon the earth. In this outpouring, Joel 2 prophesies that the Spirit of the Lord will be poured out upon all flesh and great miracles, signs, and wonders will take place in order to bring in the final harvest before Christ's return.

I believe that this revival will also see believers doing the "greater works" that Jesus promised we would do (John 14:12). Jesus' prayer in John 17 indicates to me that a time is coming when we will see a greater oneness and anointing on the Body of Christ than ever before—"that the world may know" about our Lord.

Q. Who are the 144,000 in the book of Revelation?

A. The 144,000 in the book of Revelation are those Jews, 12,000 from each of the 12 tribes of Israel (Revelation 7:4-8), who will accept Jesus as their Messiah during the Tribulation. This group is prophesied to be flaming preachers of the gospel of the Lord Jesus Christ and will evangelize the world during the Tribulation era. They, of course, will receive a special reward for their faithfulness to the Lord and their labor in Christ.

Q. Marilyn, do you really believe that the end is near—that Jesus' coming is imminent?

A. Yes, I do believe that we are living in the end times, and that Jesus will soon return for the Church in what we call the Rapture. That event will usher in the seven years of Tribulation, then Jesus will return to earth. All the end-time prophecies indicate this—that is why I am busy covering the earth with His Word.

Q. In regard to the temple that must be built before the Second Coming of Jesus, does this refer to a physical, material temple, or could it be a temple in another form—revival, a prophet, etc.?

A. The temple spoken of in Revelation 11 will be a literal temple. Israel will make a peaceful agreement with the Antichrist during the first portion of the Tribulation, and during this time the Jews will build their temple and once again offer sacrifices. In the middle of the Tribulation, the Antichrist will break this agreement and set up his idol in the temple.

Q. Where in Israel is the valley of Jehoshaphat where Christ will judge the people at the end of the Millennium?

A. The valley of Jehoshaphat is the same as Armageddon, and this is the place where Jehoshaphat achieved a great victory by sending out the praisers and worshipers before the warriors according to God's direction. When the Bible speaks of the valley of Jehoshaphat, the Jews remember this as a place of great victory and of great encouragement. (See Joel 3:2,12.)

The valley of Jehoshaphat is important to Christians because Ezekiel 38 and 39 describe the end-time battle of Armageddon. There are four groups of nations mentioned in this account. Three of the groups are under the Antichrist: (1) Meshech and Tubal (southern Russia and the area between the Black and Caspian Seas); (2) Persia (modern Iraq), Ethiopia, and Libya; and (3) Gomer and Togarmah (the nations of Europe). The fourth group of nations are mentioned in Ezekiel 38:13: "*. . . the merchants of*

Tarshish, with all the young lions thereof, ..." The merchants of Tarshish are Gibraltar, and the young lions are the offshoots of Great Britain which would include America, Canada, and Australia. These come to hinder the Antichrist and his allies at the time of Armageddon.

Q. How many beasts are there in the book of Revelation and what do they represent?

A. There are four beasts or living creatures described in Revelation 4:6-9. This passage is very similar to Ezekiel 1:10. I believe these four living creatures reflect the nature of God. The four gospels present Jesus as man (Luke), a lion (Matthew), an ox (Mark), and as an eagle (John).

In Revelation 13 two more beasts are introduced. These beasts are definitely not of God. Revelation 13:1 describes the Antichrist while verse 11 deals with the false prophet who will do signs and wonders with the Antichrist.

Q. Please explain the abomination of desolation spoken of by Daniel and referred to in Matthew 24.

A. "*Therefore when you see the ABOMINATION OF DESOLATION which was spoken of through Daniel the prophet, standing in the holy place (let the reader understand), then let those who are in Judea flee to the mountains*" (Matthew 24:15,16 NAS). In the Bible abomination usually refers to idolatry (see I Kings 11:5-7; Ezekiel 8:16,17). The abomination spoken of by Jesus in Matthew 24 is an idol set up by the Antichrist in the Holy of Holies of the rebuilt Jewish temple. It is this idol that "stands" in the holy place; Jesus instructed His followers to "flee to the mountains."

Q. I have several questions about the Antichrist. Is he alive now? Was he born like a man? Who is his unfortunate mother? Does Satan have the power to create him?

A. I do not want to be one who "sets a date" on God's end-time timetable; therefore, I cannot give you a definite answer as to whether the Antichrist is alive now. World conditions and Bible prophecy would seem to indicate he may be living at the present time, but we have no scripture to prove such a statement.

The Antichrist will be a flesh and blood man, born of a woman, who becomes the embodiment of Satan. You may read more about him in Revelation chapter 13. The Bible does not tell us anything about the mother of the Antichrist.

Satan does not have the power to create—only God has the power to create (Isaiah 44:24; Colossians 1:16). Satan will not create the Antichrist, but he will use the Antichrist to carry out his evil purposes.

Q. We know that the mark of the beast is 666. What are Christians supposed to do if our telephone number, credit cards, etc., contain these numbers?

A. There is no reason to be alarmed if your telephone number, address, or anything else contains 666. There is nothing intrinsically evil in this number. Revelation 13:16-18 tells us that 666 is a mystery number of the Antichrist. It will have no significance until the period of time during the Tribulation when people are warned not to take the "mark of the beast."

Chapter Nineteen

HOW TO STUDY THE BIBLE

Q. I want to study the Bible at home, but I don't even know how to begin. Can you give me any ideas?

A. The key to Bible study is consistency. I would suggest that you make up a Bible reading schedule for yourself or use the one that I offer in OUTPOURING magazine.

As you read, pray that the Holy Spirit will give you revelation and inspiration on what He is teaching you that day. I would encourage you to get a notebook and jot down those revelations as He gives them to you. Every insight that is important for you may be important for someone else as well. Your notes can also encourage you later when you go back and reread them.

Set aside a specific time each day when you know you won't be interrupted. Then select a topic, a character, or even a particular book to concentrate on. Or you may even want to do a chronological study of a person's life and trace how God's Word changed that person's life. (A chronological Bible is helpful for this type of study.) Begin to memorize key verses that apply to your life and circumstances. I know people who write verses down and attach them to their refrigerators, dashboards, mirrors, and even the shower wall so they can study them until they have them memorized. And above all, remain open to what the Holy Spirit may reveal to you.

I would also suggest that you study different translations of the same passage. We may often be tempted to say to ourselves, "Oh, I know what this says"; and then skip over it to something we may not have seen before. But if you read it from a different translation, God may reveal something new to you. I can't begin to tell you how many times I've ended up saying, "I've never seen *that* before in this scripture!"

Another option for you might be to go to a Bible bookstore and ask for home Bible studies there. I have a Bible study series called, "Living in Victory." These are excellent guidelines in reading for your home study.

I would also recommend that you get other reference materials to aid your study. Some of my favorite resources are STRONG'S EXHAUSTIVE CONCORDANCE—for the Hebrew and Greek word definitions; VINE'S EXPOSITORY DICTIONARY—for word studies; and DAKE'S ANNOTATED REFERENCE BIBLE—for its excellent notes. I also enjoy using HEBREW HONEY, which defines many significant Old Testament words. (You can purchase HEBREW HONEY through this ministry.)

Q. I write, mark, and underline scriptures in my Bible; and I'm wondering if it's OK to do this? I don't mean any disrespect in doing so.

A. There is nothing wrong with marking or underlining scriptures in your Bible. Second Timothy 2:15 tells us to *"Study to shew thyself approved. . . ."* I have often heard excellent Bible teachers say that if your Bible is too good to mark in, then throw it away and get one that you can mark in! So go right ahead and use your Bible—I do! I have found my notes very helpful later when I've been studying and preparing for teaching. These notes refreshed my memory from an earlier time when God gave revelation knowledge to me, and then I can pass on that knowledge to others as I teach the Word. I think you'll find that you will be blessed if you make notes as you study.

Read Through the Bible in One Year

Faithfully reading the Bible on a consistent basis has helped me grow in my walk in the Lord. I believe every Christian should read the Bible daily. If you are not already using a Bible-reading program, then here is a good one for you. By following this plan, you will be able to read through the *entire Bible* in just one year.

If you would like a short devotional to go along with each day's reading, then you will enjoy using my OUTPOURING magazine. For a free six-month subscription to OUTPOURING, use one of the coupons in the back of this book to write or call.

JANUARY

DATE	OLD TESTAMENT	NEW TESTAMENT
January 1	Genesis 1,2,3	Matthew 1
January 2	Genesis 4,5,6	Matthew 2
January 3	Genesis 7,8,9	Matthew 3
January 4	Genesis 10,11,12	Matthew 4
January 5	Genesis 13,14,15	Matthew 5:1-26
January 6	Genesis 16,17	Matthew 5:27-48
January 7	Genesis 18,19	Matthew 6:1-18
January 8	Genesis 20,21,22	Matthew 6:19-34
January 9	Job 1,2	Matthew 7
January 10	Job 3,4	Matthew 8:1-17
January 11	Job 5,6,7	Matthew 8:18-34
January 12	Job 8,9,10	Matthew 9:1-17
January 13	Job 11,12,13	Matthew 9:18-38
January 14	Job 14,15,16	Matthew 10:1-20
January 15	Job 17,18,19	Matthew 10:21-42
January 16	Job 20,21	Matthew 11
January 17	Job 22,23,24	Matthew 12:1-23
January 18	Job 25,26,27	Matthew 12:24-50
January 19	Job 28,29	Matthew 13:1-30
January 20	Job 30,31	Matthew 13:31-58
January 21	Job 32,33	Matthew 14:1-21
January 22	Job 34,35	Matthew 14:22-36
January 23	Job 36,37	Matthew 15:1-20
January 24	Job 38,39,40	Matthew 15:21-39
January 25	Job 41,42	Matthew 16
January 26	Genesis 23,24	Matthew 17
January 27	Genesis 25,26	Matthew 18:1-20
January 28	Genesis 27,28	Matthew 18:21-35

January 29	Genesis 29,30	Matthew 19
January 30	Genesis 31,32	Matthew 20:1-16
January 31	Genesis 33,34,35	Matthew 20:17-34

FEBRUARY

DATE	OLD TESTAMENT	NEW TESTAMENT
February 1	Genesis 36,37,38	Matthew 21:1-22
February 2	Genesis 39,40	Matthew 21:23-46
February 3	Genesis 41,42	Matthew 22:1-22
February 4	Genesis 43,44,45	Matthew 22:23-46
February 5	Genesis 46,47,48	Matthew 23:1-22
February 6	Genesis 49,50	Matthew 23:23-29
February 7	Exodus 1,2,3	Matthew 24:1-28
February 8	Exodus 4,5,6	Matthew 24:29-51
February 9	Exodus 7,8	Matthew 25:1-30
February 10	Exodus 9,10,11	Matthew 25:31-46
February 11	Exodus 12,13	Matthew 26:1-35
February 12	Exodus 14,15	Matthew 26:36-75
February 13	Exodus 16,17,18	Matthew 27:1-26
February 14	Exodus 19,20	Matthew 27:27-50
February 15	Exodus 21,22	Matthew 27:51-66
February 16	Exodus 23,24	Matthew 28
February 17	Exodus 25,26	Mark 1:1-22
February 18	Exodus 27,28	Mark 1:23-45
February 19	Exodus 29,30	Mark 2
February 20	Exodus 31,32,33	Mark 3:1-19
February 21	Exodus 34,35	Mark 3:20-35
February 22	Exodus 36,37,38	Mark 4:1-20
February 23	Exodus 39,40	Mark 4:21-41
February 24	Psalms 90,91; Leviticus 1,2	Mark 5:1-20
February 25	Leviticus 3,4,5	Mark 5:21-43
February 26	Leviticus 6,7	Mark 6:1-29
February 27	Leviticus 8,9,10	Mark 6:30-56
February 28	Leviticus 11,12	Mark 7:1-13

MARCH

DATE	OLD TESTAMENT	NEW TESTAMENT
March 1	Leviticus 13	Mark 7:14-37
March 2	Leviticus 14	Mark 8:1-21
March 3	Leviticus 15,16	Mark 8:22-38
March 4	Leviticus 17,18	Mark 9:1-29
March 5	Leviticus 19,20	Mark 9:30-50
March 6	Leviticus 21,22	Mark 10:1-31
March 7	Leviticus 23,24	Mark 10:32-52
March 8	Leviticus 25	Mark 11:1-18
March 9	Leviticus 26,27	Mark 11:19-33
March 10	Numbers 1,2	Mark 12:1-27
March 11	Numbers 3,4	Mark 12:28-44
March 12	Numbers 5,6	Mark 13:1-20
March 13	Numbers 7,8	Mark 13:21-37
March 14	Numbers 9,10,11	Mark 14:1-26
March 15	Numbers 12,13,14	Mark 14:27-53
March 16	Numbers 15,16	Mark 14:54-72
March 17	Numbers 17,18,19	Mark 15:1-25
March 18	Numbers 20,21,22	Mark 15:26-47
March 19	Numbers 23,24,25	Mark 16
March 20	Numbers 26,27	Luke 1:1-20
March 21	Numbers 28,29,30	Luke 1:21-38
March 22	Numbers 31,32,33	Luke 1:39-56
March 23	Numbers 34,35,36	Luke 1:57-80
March 24	Deuteronomy 1,2	Luke 2:1-24
March 25	Deuteronomy 3,4	Luke 2:25-52
March 26	Deuteronomy 5,6,7	Luke 3
March 27	Deuteronomy 8,9,10	Luke 4:1-30
March 28	Deuteronomy 11,12,13	Luke 4:31-44
March 29	Deuteronomy 14,15,16	Luke 5:1-16
March 30	Deuteronomy 17,18,19	Luke 5:17-39
March 31	Deuteronomy 20,21,22	Luke 6:1-26

APRIL

DATE	OLD TESTAMENT	NEW TESTAMENT
April 1	Deuteronomy 23,24,25	Luke 6:27-49
April 2	Deuteronomy 26,27	Luke 7:1-30
April 3	Deuteronomy 28,29	Luke 7:31-50
April 4	Deuteronomy 30,31	Luke 8:1-25
April 5	Deuteronomy 32,33,34	Luke 8:26-56
April 6	Joshua 1,2,3	Luke 9:1-17
April 7	Joshua 4,5,6	Luke 9:18-36
April 8	Joshua 7,8,9	Luke 9:37-62
April 9	Joshua 10,11,12	Luke 10:1-24
April 10	Joshua 13,14,15	Luke 10:25-42
April 11	Joshua 16,17,18	Luke 11:1-28
April 12	Joshua 19,20,21	Luke 11:29-54
April 13	Joshua 22,23,24	Luke 12:1-31
April 14	Judges 1,2,3	Luke 12:32-59
April 15	Judges 4,5,6	Luke 13:1-22
April 16	Judges 7,8	Luke 13:23-35
April 17	Judges 9,10	Luke 14:1-24
April 18	Judges 11,12	Luke 14:25-35
April 19	Judges 13,14,15	Luke 15:1-10
April 20	Judges 16,17,18	Luke 15:11-32
April 21	Judges 19,20,21	Luke 16
April 22	Ruth 1,2,3,4	Luke 17:1-19
April 23	I Samuel 1,2,3	Luke 17:20-37
April 24	I Samuel 4,5,6	Luke 18:1-23
April 25	I Samuel 7,8,9	Luke 18:24-43
April 26	I Samuel 10,11,12	Luke 19:1-27
April 27	I Samuel 13,14	Luke 19:28-48
April 28	I Samuel 15,16	Luke 20:1-26
April 29	I Samuel 17,18	Luke 20:27-47
April 30	I Samuel 19; Psalms 23,59	Luke 21:1-19

MAY

DATE	OLD TESTAMENT	NEW TESTAMENT
May 1	I Samuel 20,21; Psalms 31	Luke 21:20-38
May 2	I Samuel 22; Psalms 56	Luke 22:1-23
May 3	Psalms 52,57,142	Luke 22:24-46
May 4	I Samuel 23; Psalms 54,63	Luke 22:47-71
May 5	I Samuel 24,25,26,27	Luke 23:1-25
May 6	I Samuel 28,29	Luke 23:26-56
May 7	I Samuel 30,31	Luke 24:1-35
May 8	II Samuel 1,2	Luke 24:36-53
May 9	II Samuel 3,4,5	John 1:1-28
May 10	II Samuel 6,7; Psalms 30	John 1:29-51
May 11	II Samuel 8,9; Psalms 60	John 2
May 12	II Samuel 10,11,12	John 3:1-15
May 13	Psalms 32,51	John 3:16-36
May 14	II Samuel 13,14	John 4:1-26
May 15	II Samuel 15; Psalms 3,69	John 4:27-54
May 16	II Samuel 16,17,18	John 5:1-24
May 17	II Samuel 19,20	John 5:25-47
May 18	Psalms 64,70	John 6:1-21
May 19	II Samuel 21,22; Psalms 18	John 6:22-40
May 20	II Samuel 23,24	John 6:41-71
May 21	Psalms 4,5,6	John 7:1-27
May 22	Psalms 7,8	John 7:28-53
May 23	Psalms 9,11	John 8:1-27
May 24	Psalms 12,13,14	John 8:28-59
May 25	Psalms 15,16	John 9:1-23
May 26	Psalms 17,19	John 9:24-41
May 27	Psalms 20,21,22	John 10:1-21

May 28	Psalms 24,25,26	John 10:22-42
May 29	Psalms 27,28,29	John 11:1-29
May 30	Psalms 34,35	John 11:30-57
May 31	Psalms 36,37,38	John 12:1-26

JUNE

DATE	OLD TESTAMENT	NEW TESTAMENT
June 1	Psalms 39,40,41	John 12:27-50
June 2	Psalms 53,55,58	John 13:1-20
June 3	Psalms 61,62,65	John 13:21-38
June 4	Psalms 68,72,86	John 14
June 5	Psalms 101,103,108	John 15
June 6	Psalms 109,110,138	John 16
June 7	Psalms 139,140,141	John 17
June 8	Psalms 143,144,145	John 18:1-18
June 9	I Kings 1,2	John 18:19-40
June 10	I Kings 3,4; Proverbs 1	John 19:1-22
June 11	Proverbs 2,3,4	John 19:23-42
June 12	Proverbs 5,6,7	John 20
June 13	Proverbs 8,9	John 21
June 14	Proverbs 10,11,12	Acts 1
June 15	Proverbs 13,14,15	Acts 2:1-21
June 16	Proverbs 16,17,18	Acts 2:22-47
June 17	Proverbs 19,20,21	Acts 3
June 18	Proverbs 22,23,24	Acts 4:1-22
June 19	Proverbs 25,26	Acts 4:23-37
June 20	Proverbs 27,28,29	Acts 5:1-21
June 21	Proverbs 30,31	Acts 5:22-42
June 22	Song of Solomon 1,2,3	Acts 6
June 23	Song of Solomon 4,5	Acts 7:1-21
June 24	Song of Solomon 6,7,8	Acts 7:22-43
June 25	I Kings 5,6,7	Acts 7:44-60
June 26	I Kings 8,9	Acts 8:1-25
June 27	I Kings 10,11	Acts 8:26-40

June 28	Ecclesiastes 1,2,3	Acts 9:1-22
June 29	Ecclesiastes 4,5,6	Acts 9:23-43
June 30	Ecclesiastes 7,8,9	Acts 10:1-23

JULY

DATE	**OLD TESTAMENT**	**NEW TESTAMENT**
July 1	Ecclesiastes 10,11,12	Acts 10:24-48
July 2	I Kings 12,13	Acts 11
July 3	I Kings 14,15	Acts 12
July 4	I Kings 16,17,18	Acts 13:1-25
July 5	I Kings 19,20	Acts 13:26-52
July 6	I Kings 21,22	Acts 14
July 7	II Kings 1,2,3	James 1
July 8	II Kings 4,5,6	James 2
July 9	II Kings 7,8,9	James 3
July 10	II Kings 10,11,12	James 4
July 11	II Kings 13,14	James 5
July 12	Jonah 1,2,3,4	Acts 15:1-21
July 13	Amos 1,2,3	Acts 15:22-41
July 14	Amos 4,5,6	Galatians 1
July 15	Amos 7,8,9	Galatians 2
July 16	II Kings 15,16	Galatians 3
July 17	II Kings 17,18	Galatians 4
July 18	II Kings 19,20,21	Galatians 5
July 19	II Kings 22,23	Galatians 6
July 20	II Kings 24,25	Acts 16:1-21
July 21	Psalms 1,2,10	Acts 16:22-40
July 22	Psalms 33,43,66	Philippians 1
July 23	Psalms 67,71	Philippians 2
July 24	Psalms 89,92	Philippians 3
July 25	Psalms 93,94,95	Philippians 4
July 26	Psalms 96,97,98	Acts 17:1-15
July 27	Psalms 99,100,102	Acts 17:16-34
July 28	Psalms 104,105	I Thessalonians 1
July 29	Psalms 106,111,112	I Thessalonians 2
July 30	Psalms 113,114,115	I Thessalonians 3

July 31	Psalms 116,117,118	I Thessalonians 4

AUGUST

DATE	**OLD TESTAMENT**	**NEW TESTAMENT**
August 1	Psalms 119:1-88	I Thessalonians 5
August 2	Psalms 119:89-176	II Thessalonians 1
August 3	Psalms 120,121,122	II Thessalonians 2
August 4	Psalms 123,124,125	II Thessalonians 3
August 5	Psalms 127,128,129	Acts 18
August 6	Psalms 130,131,132	I Corinthians 1
August 7	Psalms 133,134,135	I Corinthians 2
August 8	Psalms 136,146	I Corinthians 3
August 9	Psalms 147,148	I Corinthians 4
August 10	Psalms 149,150	I Corinthians 5
August 11	I Chronicles 1,2,3	I Corinthians 6
August 12	I Chronicles 4,5,6	I Corinthians 7:1-19
August 13	I Chronicles 7,8,9	I Corinthians 7:20-40
August 14	I Chronicles 10,11,12	I Corinthians 8
August 15	I Chronicles 13,14,15	I Corinthians 9
August 16	I Chronicles 16; Psalms 42,44	I Corinthians 10:1-18
August 17	Psalms 45,46,47	I Corinthians 10:19-33
August 18	Psalms 48,49,50	I Corinthians 11:1-16
August 19	Psalms 73,85	I Corinthians 11:17-34
August 20	Psalms 87,88	I Corinthians 12
August 21	I Chronicles 17,18,19	I Corinthians 13
August 22	I Chronicles 20,21,22	I Corinthians 14:1-20
August 23	I Chronicles 23,24,25	I Corinthians 14:21-40
August 24	I Chronicles 26,27	I Corinthians 15:1-28
August 25	I Chronicles 28,29	I Corinthians 15:29-58
August 26	II Chronicles 1,2,3	I Corinthians 16
August 27	II Chronicles 4,5,6	II Corinthians 1
August 28	II Chronicles 7,8,9	II Corinthians 2
August 29	II Chronicles 10,11,12	II Corinthians 3
August 30	II Chronicles 13,14	II Corinthians 4
August 31	II Chronicles 15,16	II Corinthians 5

SEPTEMBER

DATE	OLD TESTAMENT	NEW TESTAMENT
September 1	II Chronicles 17,18	II Corinthians 6
September 2	II Chronicles 19,20	II Corinthians 7
September 3	II Chronicles 21; Obadiah	II Corinthians 8
September 4	II Chronicles 22; Joel 1	II Corinthians 9
September 5	II Chronicles 23; Joel 2,3	II Corinthians 10
September 6	II Chronicles 24,25,26	II Corinthians 11:1-15
September 7	Isaiah 1,2	II Corinthians 11:16-33
September 8	Isaiah 3,4	II Corinthians 12
September 9	Isaiah 5,6	II Corinthians 13
September 10	II Chronicles 27,28	Acts 19:1-20
September 11	II Chronicles 29,30	Acts 19:21-41
September 12	II Chronicles 31,32	Acts 20:1-16
September 13	Isaiah 7,8	Acts 20:17-38
September 14	Isaiah 9,10	Ephesians 1
September 15	Isaiah 11,12,13	Ephesians 2
September 16	Isaiah 14,15,16	Ephesians 3
September 17	Isaiah 17,18,19	Ephesians 4
September 18	Isaiah 20,21,22	Ephesians 5:1-16
September 19	Isaiah 23,24,25	Ephesians 5:17-33
September 20	Isaiah 26,27	Ephesians 6
September 21	Isaiah 28,29	Romans 1
September 22	Isaiah 30,31	Romans 2
September 23	Isaiah 32,33	Romans 3
September 24	Isaiah 34,35,36	Romans 4
September 25	Isaiah 37,38	Romans 5
September 26	Isaiah 39,40	Romans 6
September 27	Isaiah 41,42	Romans 7
September 28	Isaiah 43,44	Romans 8:1-21
September 29	Isaiah 45,46	Romans 8:22-39
September 30	Isaiah 47,48,49	Romans 9:1-15

OCTOBER

DATE	OLD TESTAMENT	NEW TESTAMENT
October 1	Isaiah 50,51,52	Romans 9:16-33
October 2	Isaiah 53,54,55	Romans 10
October 3	Isaiah 56,57,58	Romans 11:1-18
October 4	Isaiah 59,60,61	Romans 11:19-36
October 5	Isaiah 62,63,64	Romans 12
October 6	Isaiah 65,66	Romans 13
October 7	Hosea 1,2,3,4	Romans 14
October 8	Hosea 5,6,7,8	Romans 15:1-13
October 9	Hosea 9,10,11	Romans 15:14-33
October 10	Hosea 12,13,14	Romans 16
October 11	Micah 1,2,3	Acts 21:1-17
October 12	Micah 4,5	Acts 21:18-40
October 13	Micah 6,7	Acts 22
October 14	Nahum 1,2,3	Acts 23:1-15
October 15	II Chronicles 33,34	Acts 23:16-35
October 16	Zephaniah 1,2,3	Acts 24
October 17	II Chronicles 35; Habukkuk 1,2,3	Acts 25
October 18	Jeremiah 1,2	Acts 26
October 19	Jeremiah 3,4,5	Acts 27:1-26
October 20	Jeremiah 6,11,12	Acts 27:27-44
October 21	Jeremiah 7,8,26	Acts 28
October 22	Jeremiah 9,10,14	Colossians 1
October 23	Jeremiah 15,16,17	Colossians 2
October 24	Jeremiah 18,19	Colossians 3
October 25	Jeremiah 20,35,36	Colossians 4
October 26	Jeremiah 25,45,46	Hebrews 1
October 27	Jeremiah 47,48	Hebrews 2
October 28	Jeremiah 49,13,22	Hebrews 3
October 29	Jeremiah 23,24	Hebrews 4
October 30	Jeremiah 27,28,29	Hebrews 5
October 31	Jeremiah 50	Hebrews 6

NOVEMBER

DATE	OLD TESTAMENT	NEW TESTAMENT
November 1	Jeremiah 51,30	Hebrews 7
November 2	Jeremiah 31,32	Hebrews 8
November 3	Jeremiah 33,21	Hebrews 9
November 4	Jeremiah 34,37,38	Hebrews 10:1-18
November 5	Jeremiah 39,52,40	Hebrews 10:19-39
November 6	Jeremiah 41,42	Hebrews 11:1-19
November 7	Jeremiah 43,44	Hebrews 11:20-40
November 8	Lamentations 1,2	Hebrews 12
November 9	Lamentations 3,4,5	Hebrews 13
November 10	II Chronicles 36; Daniel 1,2	Titus 1
November 11	Daniel 3,4	Titus 2
November 12	Daniel 5,6,7	Titus 3
November 13	Daniel 8,9,10	Philemon
November 14	Daniel 11,12	I Timothy 1
November 15	Psalms 137; Ezekiel 1,2	I Timothy 2
November 16	Ezekiel 3,4	I Timothy 3
November 17	Ezekiel 5,6,7	I Timothy 4
November 18	Ezekiel 8,9,10	I Timothy 5
November 19	Ezekiel 11,12,13	I Timothy 6
November 20	Ezekiel 14,15	II Timothy 1
November 21	Ezekiel 16,17	II Timothy 2
November 22	Ezekiel 18,19	II Timothy 3
November 23	Ezekiel 20,21	II Timothy 4
November 24	Ezekiel 22,23	I Peter 1
November 25	Ezekiel 24,25,26	I Peter 2
November 26	Ezekiel 27,28,29	I Peter 3
November 27	Ezekiel 30,31,32	I Peter 4
November 28	Ezekiel 33,34	I Peter 5
November 29	Ezekiel 35,36	II Peter 1
November 30	Ezekiel 37,38,39	II Peter 2

DECEMBER

DATE	OLD TESTAMENT	NEW TESTAMENT
December 1	Ezekiel 40,41	II Peter 3
December 2	Ezekiel 42,43,44	I John 1
December 3	Ezekiel 45,46	I John 2
December 4	Ezekiel 47,48	I John 3
December 5	Ezra 1,2	I John 4
December 6	Ezra 3,4	I John 5
December 7	Haggai 1,2	II John
December 8	Zechariah 1,2,3,4	III John
December 9	Zechariah 5,6,7,8	Jude
December 10	Zechariah 9,10	Revelation 1
December 11	Zechariah 11,12	Revelation 2
December 12	Zechariah 13,14	Revelation 3,4
December 13	Psalms 74,75,76	Revelation 5
December 14	Psalms 77,78	Revelation 6
December 15	Psalms 79,80	Revelation 7
December 16	Psalms 81,82	Revelation 8
December 17	Psalms 83,84	Revelation 9
December 18	Psalms 107,126	Revelation 10
December 19	Ezra 5,6,7	Revelation 11
December 20	Esther 1,2	Revelation 12
December 21	Esther 3,4,5	Revelation 13
December 22	Esther 6,7,8	Revelation 14
December 23	Esther 9,10	Revelation 15
December 24	Ezra 8,9,10	Revelation 16
December 25	Nehemiah 1,2,3	Matthew 1; Luke 2
December 26	Nehemiah 4,5,6	Revelation 17
December 27	Nehemiah 7,8,9	Revelation 18
December 28	Nehemiah 10,11	Revelation 19
December 29	Nehemiah 12,13	Revelation 20
December 30	Malachi 1,2	Revelation 21
December 31	Malachi 3,4	Revelation 22

Receive Jesus Christ as Lord and Savior of Your Life.

The Bible says, *"That if thou shalt confess with thy mouth the Lord Jesus, and shalt believe in thine heart that God hath raised him from the dead, thou shalt be saved. For with the heart man believeth unto righteousness; and with the mouth confession is made unto salvation"* (Romans 10:9,10).

To receive Jesus Christ as Lord and Savior of your life, sincerely pray this prayer from your heart:

Dear Jesus,

I believe that You died for me and that You rose again on the third day. I confess to You that I am a sinner and that I need Your love and forgiveness. Come into my life, forgive my sins, and give me eternal life. I confess You now as my Lord. Thank You for my salvation!

Signed ______________________________

Date ______________________________

Write to us.

We will send you information to help you with your new life in Christ.

Marilyn Hickey Ministries • P.O. Box 17340
Denver, CO 80217 • (303) 770-0400

Prayer Request(s)

Let us join our faith with yours for your prayer needs. Fill out the coupon below and send to Marilyn Hickey Ministries, P.O. Box 17340, Denver, CO 80217.

Prayer Request(s) ______________________________

____

____

____

____

____

Mr. & Mrs.
Mr.
Miss
Mrs.

Please print.

Name ______________________________________

Address ____________________________________

City _______________________________________

State _____________________ Zip ____________

Phone(H) (   ) ___________________________

(W) (   ) ___________________________

If you want prayer immediately, call our Prayer Center at (303) 796-1333, Monday-Friday, 4 a.m. - 4:30 p.m. (MT).

BOOKS BY MARILYN HICKEY

A Cry for Miracles ($7.95)
Acts of the Holy Spirit ($7.95)
Angels All Around ($7.95)
Armageddon ($4.95)
Ask Marilyn ($9.95)
Be Healed ($9.95)
Blessing Journal ($4.95)
Bible Encounter Classic Edition ($24.95)
Book of Revelation Comic Book (The) ($3.00)
Break the Generation Curse ($7.95)
Break the Generation Curse Part 2 ($9.95)
Building Blocks for Better Families ($4.95)
Daily Devotional ($7.95)
Dear Marilyn ($7.95)
Devils, Demons, and Deliverance ($9.95)
Divorce Is Not the Answer ($7.95)
Especially for Today's Woman ($14.95)
Freedom From Bondages ($7.95)
Gift-Wrapped Fruit ($2.95)
God's Covenant for Your Family ($7.95)
God's Rx for a Hurting Heart ($4.95)
Hebrew Honey ($14.95)
How to Be a Mature Christian ($7.95)
Know Your Ministry ($4.95)
Maximize Your Day . . . God's Way ($7.95)
Miracle Signs and Wonders ($24.95)
Names of God (The) ($7.95)
Nehemiah—Rebuilding the Broken Places in Your Life ($7.95)
No. 1 Key to Success—Meditation (The) ($4.95)
Proverbs Classic Library Edition ($24.95)
Release the Power of the Blood Covenant ($4.95)
Satan-Proof Your Home ($7.95)
Save the Family Promise Book ($14.95)
Signs in the Heavens ($7.95)
What Every Person Wants to Know About Prayer ($4.95)
When Only a Miracle Will Do ($4.95)
Your Miracle Source ($4.95)
Your Total Health Handbook—Body • Soul • Spirit ($9.95)

MINI-BOOKS: 1^{00} each
by Marilyn Hickey

Beat Tension
Bold Men Win
Bulldog Faith
Change Your Life
Children Who Hit the Mark
Conquering Setbacks
Don't Park Here
Experience Long Life
Fasting and Prayer
God's Benefit: Healing
God's Seven Keys to Make You Rich
Hold On to Your Dream
How to Become More Than a Conqueror
How to Win Friends
I Can Be Born Again and Spirit Filled
I Can Dare to Be an Achiever
Keys to Healing Rejection
Power of Forgiveness (The)
Power of the Blood (The)
Receiving Resurrection Power
Renew Your Mind
Solving Life's Problems
Speak the Word
Standing in the Gap
Story of Esther (The)
Tithes • Offerings • Alms • God's Plan for Blessing You
Turning Point
Winning Over Weight
Women of the Word

Prices are in U.S. dollars. If ordering in foreign currency, please calculate the current exchange rate.

Marilyn Hickey Ministries

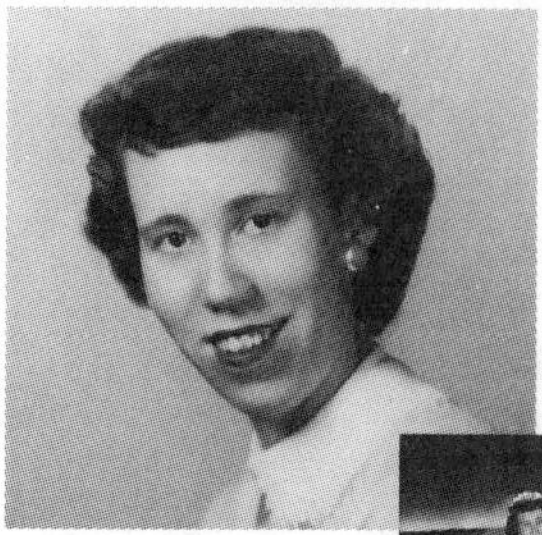

Marilyn was a public school teacher when she met Wallace Hickey. After their marriage, Wally was called to the ministry and Marilyn began teaching home Bible studies.

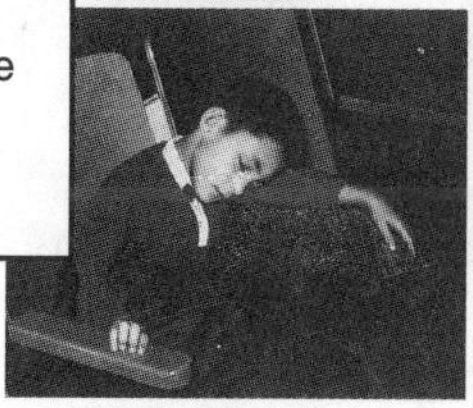

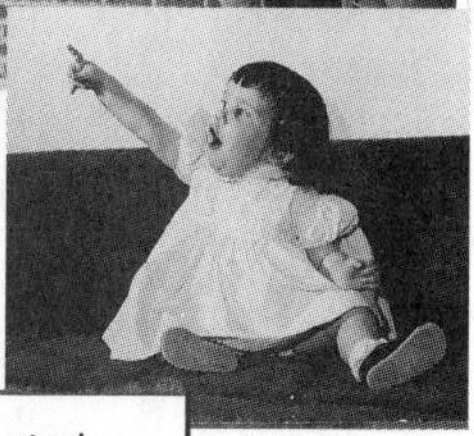

The vision of Marilyn Hickey Ministries is to "cover the earth with the Word" (Isaiah 11:9). For over 30 years Marilyn Hickey has dedicated herself to an anointed, unique, and distinguished ministry of reaching out to people—from all walks of life—who are hungry for God's Word and all that He has for them. Millions have witnessed and acclaimed the positive, personal impact she brings through fresh revelation knowledge that God has given her through His Word.

Marilyn has been the invited guest of government leaders and heads of state from many nations of the world. She is considered by many to be one of today's greatest ambassadors of God's Good News to this dark and hurting generation.

The more Marilyn follows God's will for her life, the more God uses her to bring refreshing, renewal, and revival to the Body of Christ throughout the world. As His obedient servant, Marilyn desires to follow Him all the days of her life.

Marilyn and Wally adopted their son Michael; through a fulfilled prophecy they had their daughter Sarah, who with her husband Reece, is now part of the ministry.

Marilyn founded her ministry "Life for Laymen" so that she could reach more people with her gift for practical Bible application.

Marilyn taught at Denver's "Happy Church" and hosted ministry conferences with husband Wally.

At a retreat in 1976, Marilyn realized she was called to "cover the earth with the Word."

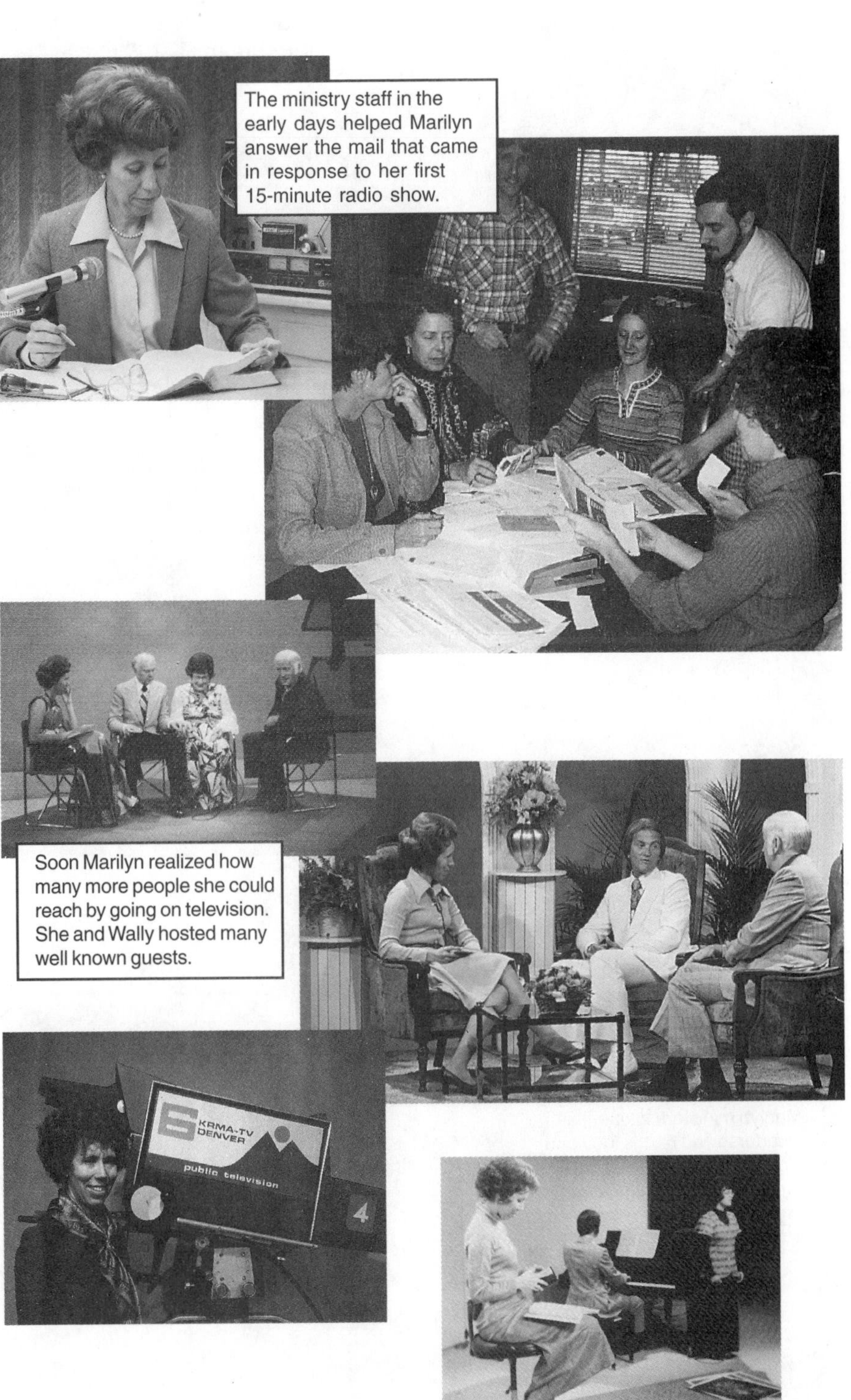

The ministry staff in the early days helped Marilyn answer the mail that came in response to her first 15-minute radio show.

Soon Marilyn realized how many more people she could reach by going on television. She and Wally hosted many well known guests.

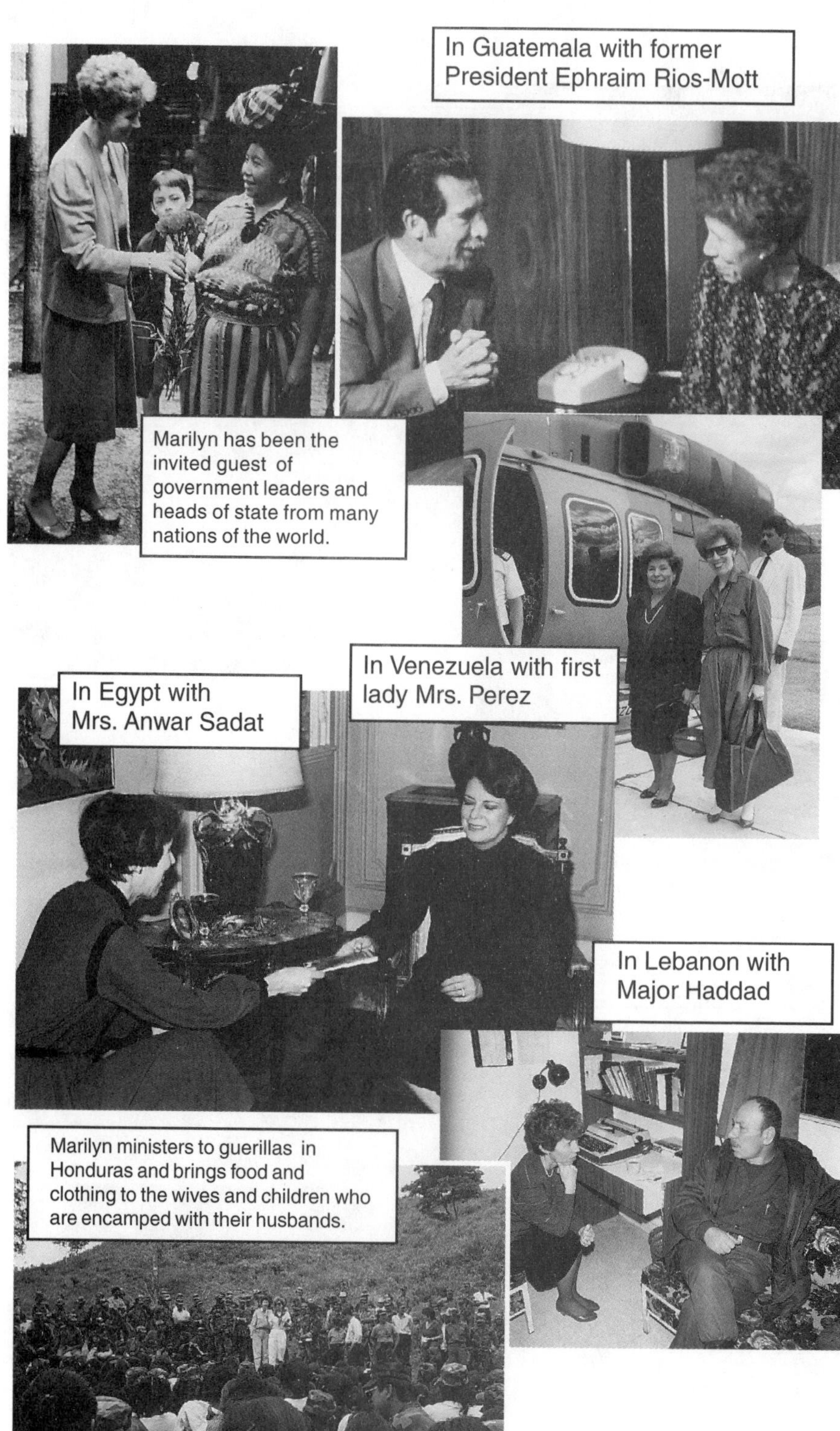

In Guatemala with former President Ephraim Rios-Mott

Marilyn has been the invited guest of government leaders and heads of state from many nations of the world.

In Venezuela with first lady Mrs. Perez

In Egypt with Mrs. Anwar Sadat

In Lebanon with Major Haddad

Marilyn ministers to guerillas in Honduras and brings food and clothing to the wives and children who are encamped with their husbands.

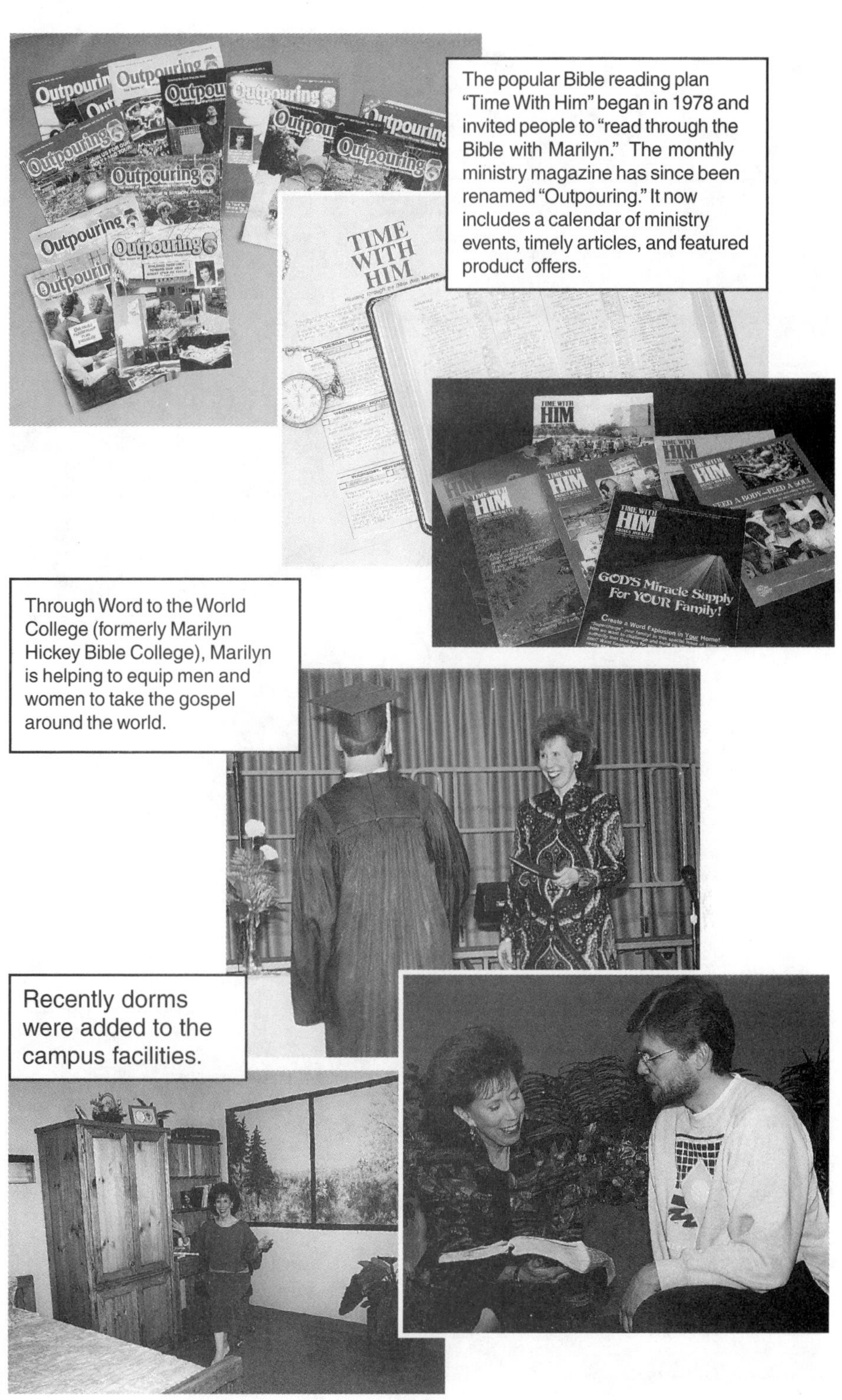

The popular Bible reading plan "Time With Him" began in 1978 and invited people to "read through the Bible with Marilyn." The monthly ministry magazine has since been renamed "Outpouring." It now includes a calendar of ministry events, timely articles, and featured product offers.

Through Word to the World College (formerly Marilyn Hickey Bible College), Marilyn is helping to equip men and women to take the gospel around the world.

Recently dorms were added to the campus facilities.

National Women's Conferences and Pastor's Wives' Conventions were held across the U.S., exhorting women to "Change Their World!"

God began to open doors for the supplying of Bibles to many foreign lands—China, Israel, Poland, Ethiopia, Russia, Romania, and Ukraine, just to name a few.

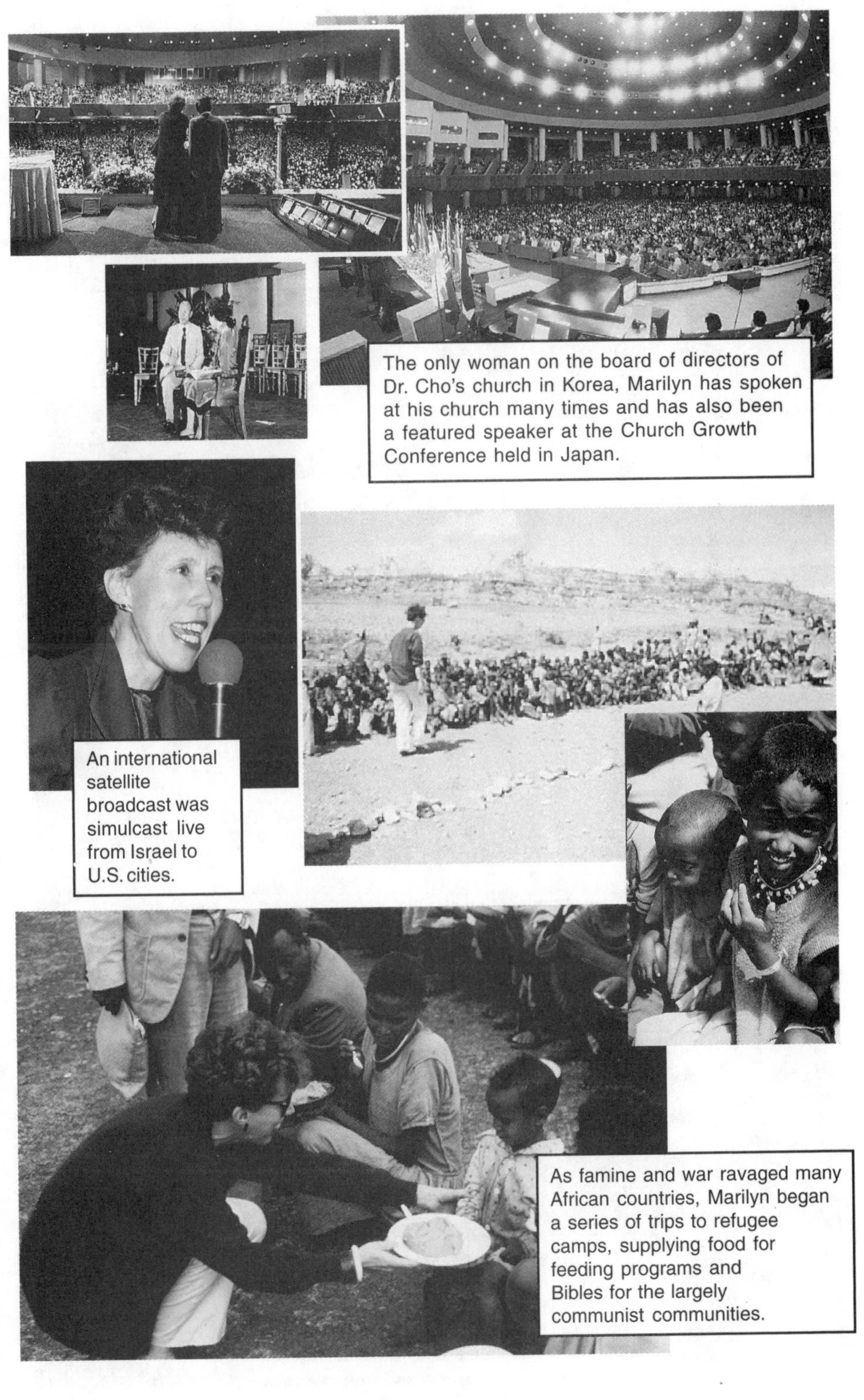

The only woman on the board of directors of Dr. Cho's church in Korea, Marilyn has spoken at his church many times and has also been a featured speaker at the Church Growth Conference held in Japan.

An international satellite broadcast was simulcast live from Israel to U.S. cities.

As famine and war ravaged many African countries, Marilyn began a series of trips to refugee camps, supplying food for feeding programs and Bibles for the largely communist communities.

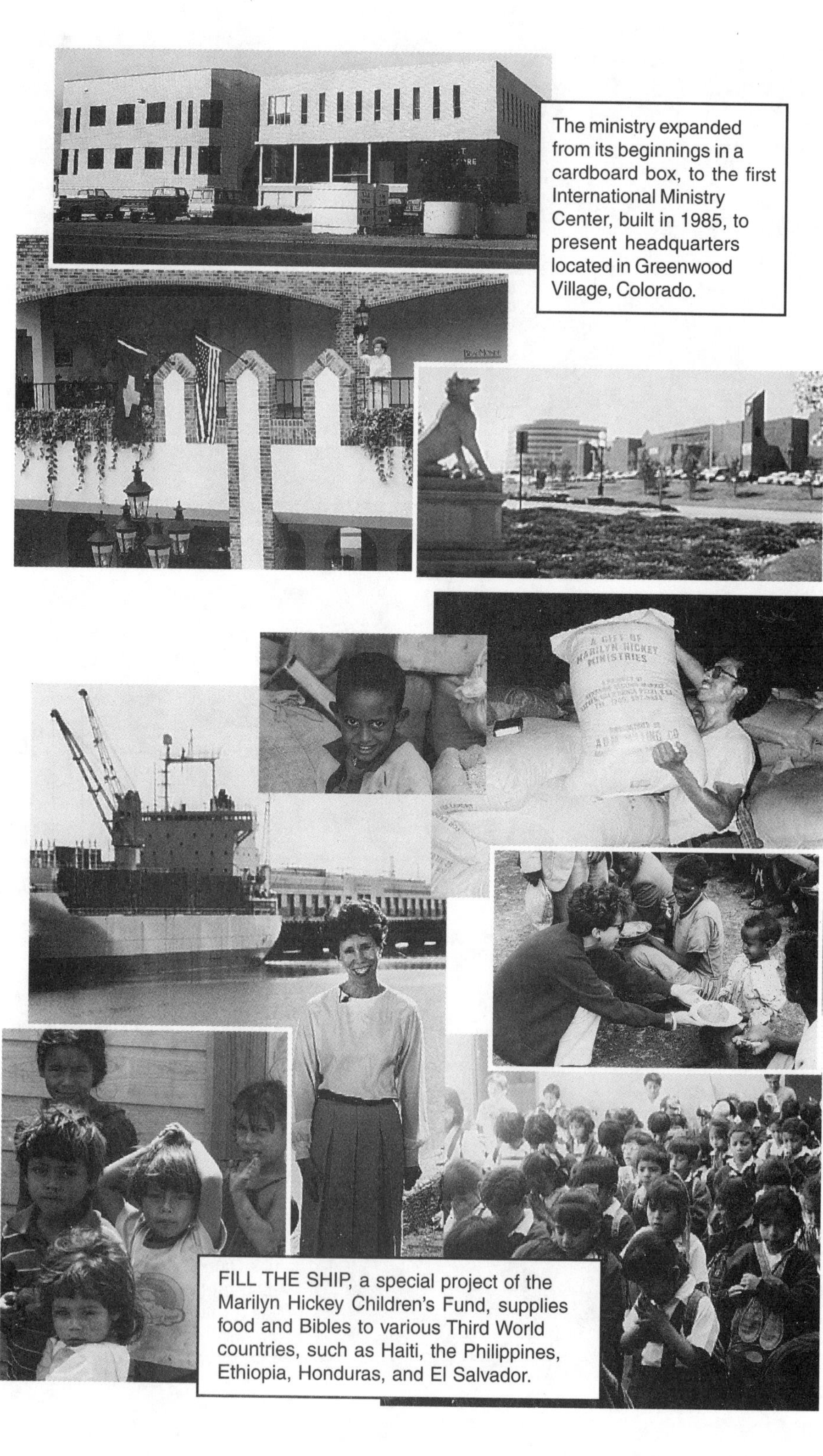

The ministry expanded from its beginnings in a cardboard box, to the first International Ministry Center, built in 1985, to present headquarters located in Greenwood Village, Colorado.

FILL THE SHIP, a special project of the Marilyn Hickey Children's Fund, supplies food and Bibles to various Third World countries, such as Haiti, the Philippines, Ethiopia, Honduras, and El Salvador.

The prime time television special, "A Cry for Miracles," featured co-host Gavin MacLeod.

Over 1,500 ministry products help people in all areas of their life.

Marilyn Hickey's Prayer Center handles calls from all over the U.S.—ministering to those who need agreement in prayer.

Marilyn ministered in underground churches in Romania before any of the European communist countries were officially open.

Ministry and speaking engagement at a Women's Conference in Nigeria

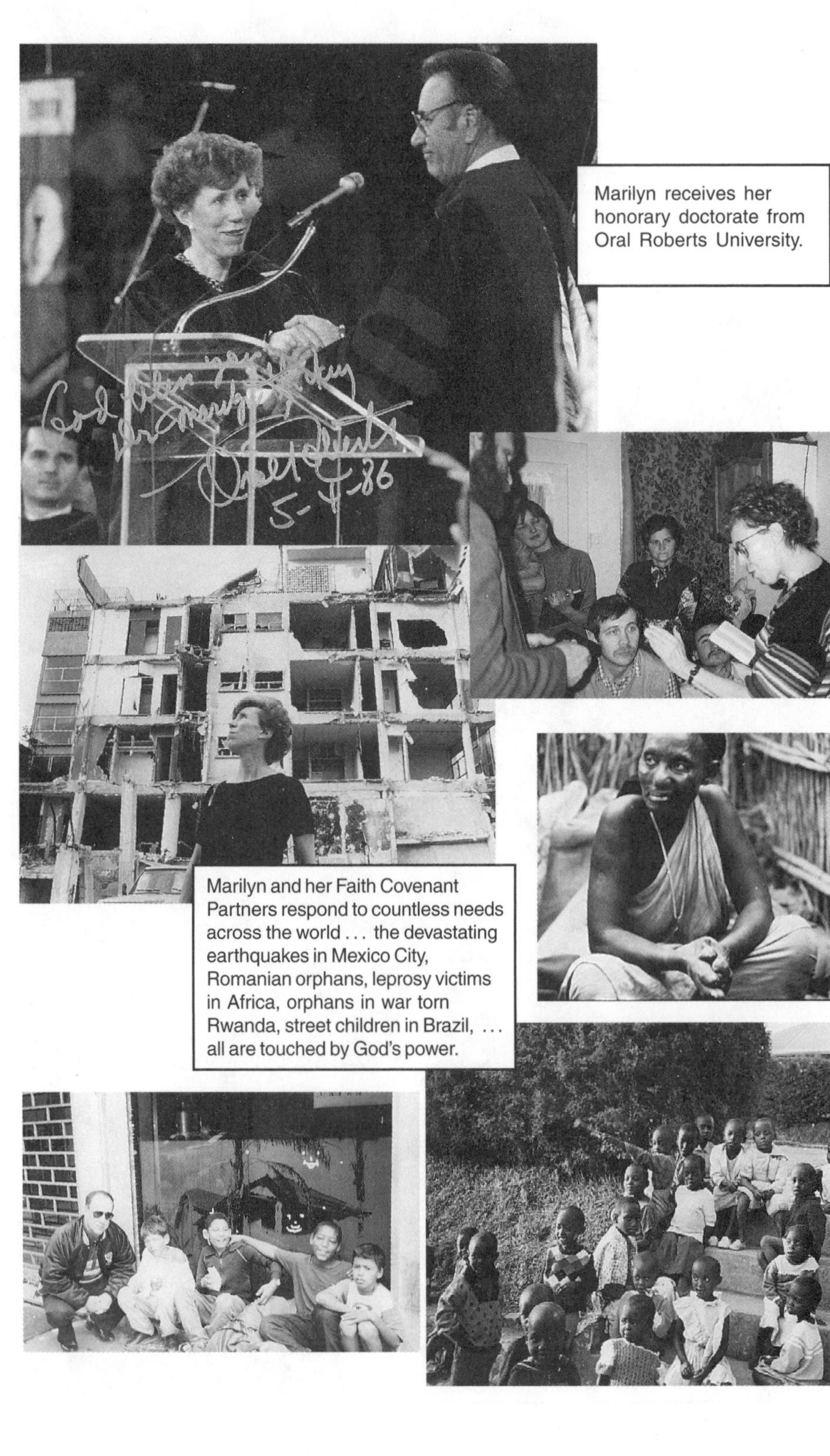

Marilyn receives her honorary doctorate from Oral Roberts University.

Marilyn and her Faith Covenant Partners respond to countless needs across the world . . . the devastating earthquakes in Mexico City, Romanian orphans, leprosy victims in Africa, orphans in war torn Rwanda, street children in Brazil, . . . all are touched by God's power.

Marilyn has been a guest several times on the 700 Club with host Pat Robertson.

Airlift Manila provided much needed food, Bibles, and personal supplies to the Philippines; MHM also raised funds to aid in the digging of water wells for those without clean drinking water.

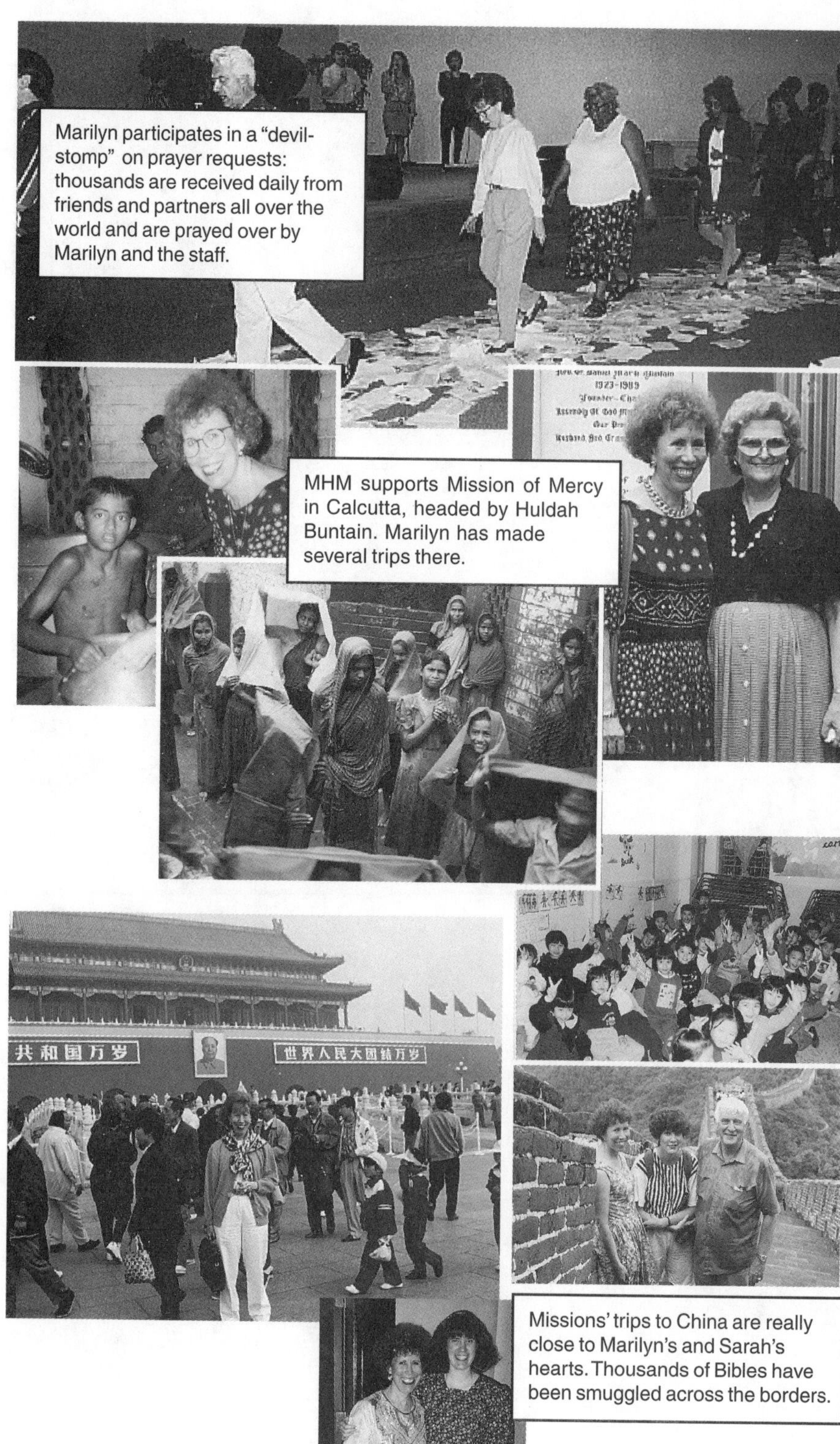

Marilyn participates in a "devil-stomp" on prayer requests: thousands are received daily from friends and partners all over the world and are prayed over by Marilyn and the staff.

MHM supports Mission of Mercy in Calcutta, headed by Huldah Buntain. Marilyn has made several trips there.

Missions' trips to China are really close to Marilyn's and Sarah's hearts. Thousands of Bibles have been smuggled across the borders.

"Today With Marilyn" Bible teaching program is broadcast weekdays on TBN, BET, and several independent stations. The program is also seen overseas by millions through Christian Network TV, in Australia on Network 10, and in more than 80 other countries worldwide.

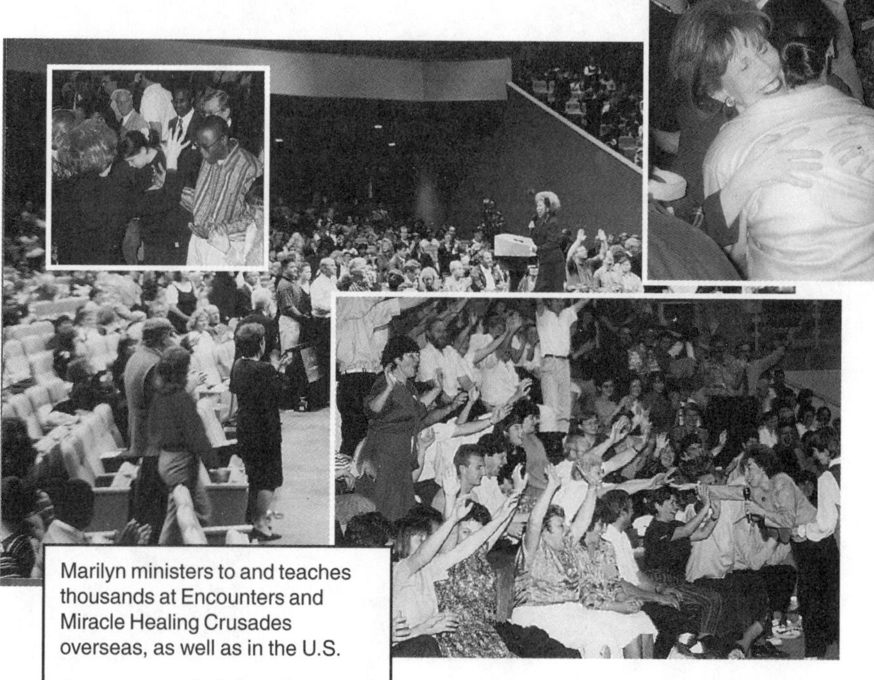

Marilyn ministers to and teaches thousands at Encounters and Miracle Healing Crusades overseas, as well as in the U.S.

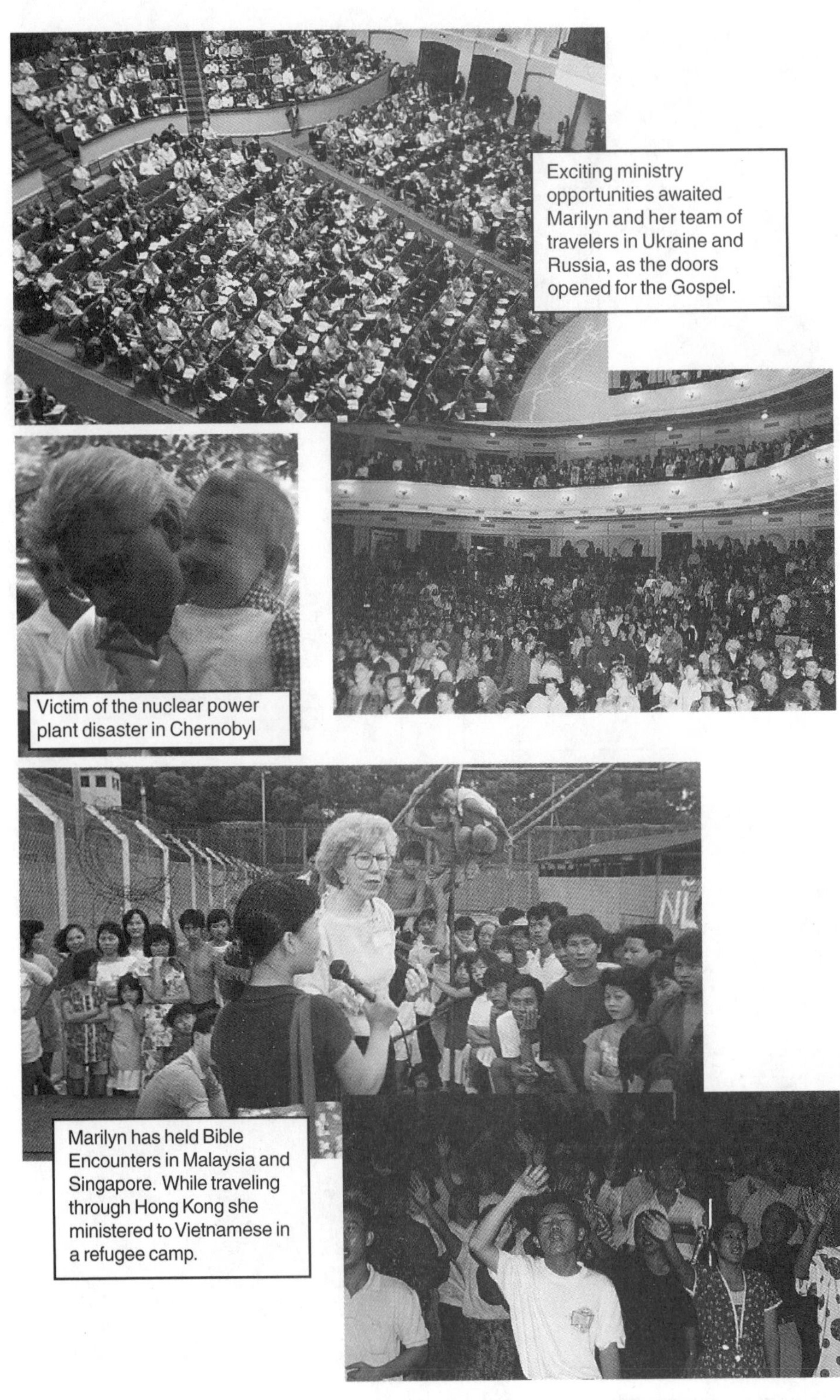
Exciting ministry opportunities awaited Marilyn and her team of travelers in Ukraine and Russia, as the doors opened for the Gospel.

Victim of the nuclear power plant disaster in Chernobyl

Marilyn has held Bible Encounters in Malaysia and Singapore. While traveling through Hong Kong she ministered to Vietnamese in a refugee camp.

Ministry trips and cruises to places such as Indonesia, Russia, Greece, Ukraine, Turkey, and Israel offer short-term missions' opportunities to travel with Marilyn to exotic places.

Overseas offices have recently been set up in the United Kingdom, Australia, and South Africa. Marilyn also hosts yearly meetings, crusades, and missions' projects in those countries.

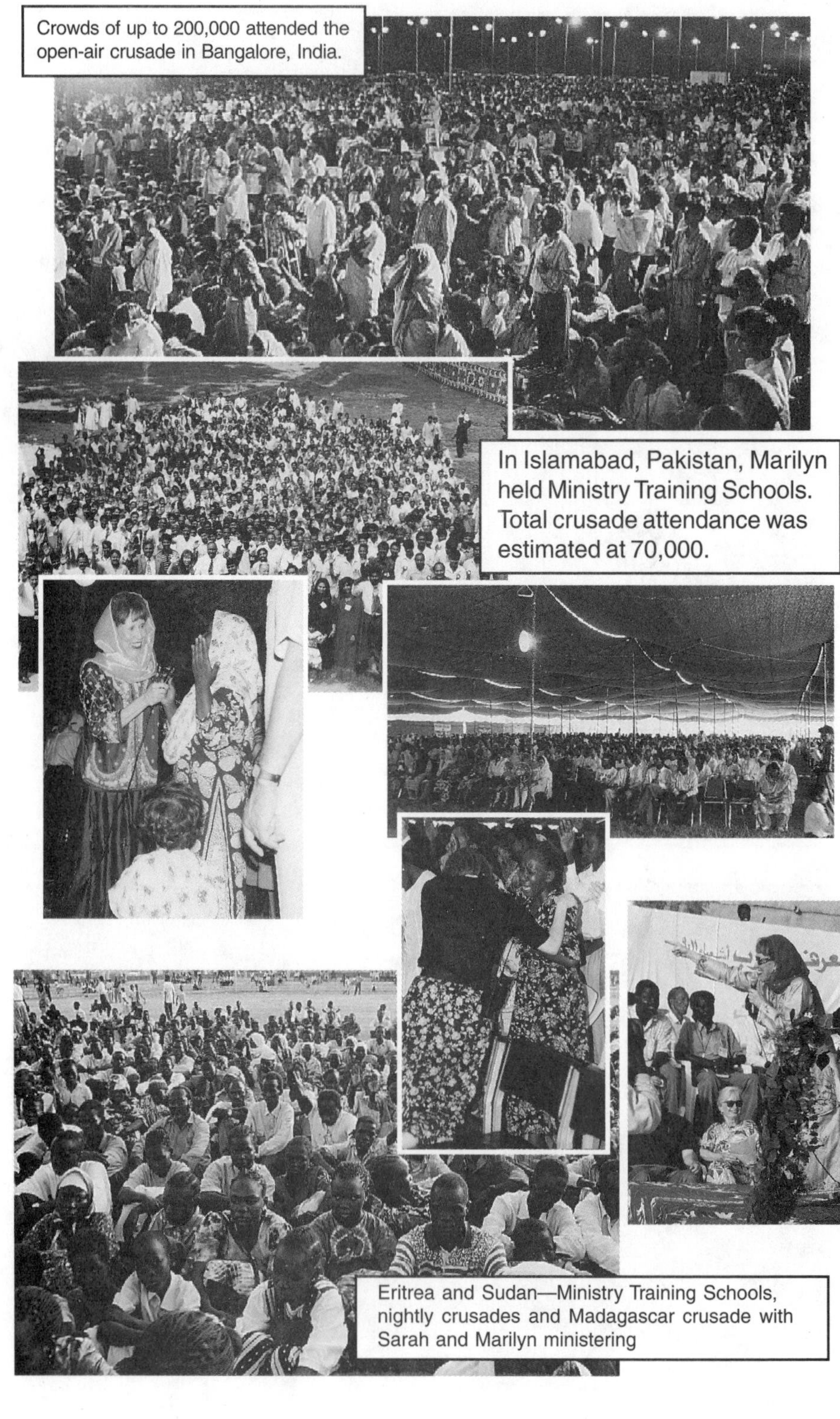

Crowds of up to 200,000 attended the open-air crusade in Bangalore, India.

In Islamabad, Pakistan, Marilyn held Ministry Training Schools. Total crusade attendance was estimated at 70,000.

Eritrea and Sudan—Ministry Training Schools, nightly crusades and Madagascar crusade with Sarah and Marilyn ministering